How to Write

by

Herbert E. Meyer

and

Jill M. Meyer

STORM KING PRESS

WASHINGTON D.C.

Storm King Press books are available at special discounts for bulk purchases for sales, promotions, premiums, fund raising or non-profit educational use. Special editions or book excerpts can also be created to specifications. For details contact:

Storm King Press
P.O. Box 3566
Washington, D.C. 20007

Tel: (202) 944-4224

Manufactured in the United States

ISBN 0-935166-01-7

For Tom and Anna

TABLE OF CONTENTS

INTRODUCTION

Let's begin by setting aside a myth: that the way to write is to sit for hours on end at a desk or a kitchen table, staring at a blank piece of paper or computer screen and waiting patiently — sometimes desperately — for inspiration to strike. Nonsense. In real life it never happens this way. Never. Not even for the best and most successful professional writers. It only looks this way because the key decisions a writer needs to make, and the steps that he or she then must take to turn these decisions into words, sentences, paragraphs, pages, and so forth, are invisible to people who haven't been shown what these decisions are and how to take the various steps that follow.

In fact, writing is less of an art than a process. And like any process, this one involves a series of decisions and steps that, when done in the correct order and with reasonable attention to detail, just about guarantee a decent and acceptable result. Happily, it isn't very difficult to make these key decisions that the writing process requires. And neither is it all that hard to take the steps that turn these decisions into polished, finished prose. The trick to writing lies in knowing what these decisions are, recognizing just what steps these decisions will require you to take next, and mastering the techniques and procedures to do it all efficiently.

This handbook is designed to help you write by showing you first, the key decisions and steps all writers need to make and, second, the skills and techniques that will turn these decisions and steps into finished, polished prose. In other words, this handbook is designed to show you how to write. For regardless of what language you speak, and regardless of what it is you're writing — a report, a letter, a memo, an essay, a book, or whatever — the writing process is always the same. Without a grasp of this process, you will have trouble writing anything, in any language; with a grasp of this process, you will be able to write anything you need or want to write, in whatever language you speak.

This handbook is designed for everyone who needs

or wants to write, including business executives, lawyers, doctors, administrators, managers, scientists, engineers, technicians, and students at all levels. It is designed to help those of you who become paralyzed by the very thought of writing, those of you who write easily but who are unable to focus what you write so that your readers can grasp your point, and those of you who just struggle along, wondering if there isn't a better way.

There certainly is a better way, and you need only turn the page to find it.

HOW TO USE THIS BOOK

This book, like the writing process itself, is divided into three parts:

—Organizing For the Job
—Turning Out a Draft
—Polishing The Product

It doesn't matter what it is you're writing. You always work your way through all three parts, and you always do it in the same order. Of course, if you're writing something short and simple like a thank-you note for a birthday gift, you won't need to spend a whole lot of time organizing for the job. However, you will likely need to spend much if not most of your time looking for just the right words to express your gratitude, which is to say turning out a first draft and then polishing the product. On the other hand, should you be writing, say, a history of World War I, organizing for the job could take years. Indeed, it will probably take longer to organize — that is, to do your research — than it will to turn out a draft and then polish the product.

Moreover, different writers have different strengths and weaknesses. Some people are especially good organizers; their problem is turning what they've organized into words on paper or on a computer diskette. Other people organize badly but write well; when these people sit down to turn out a first draft, the words flow smoothly but they find they just can't focus their thoughts. And still others always manage to turn out so-so drafts, but can't figure out how to complete the job. So different writers need to spend different percentages of their time and effort on the three parts of the writing process. The point to keep in mind is that whatever your writing project — and whatever your personal strengths and weaknesses — you will need to perform all three parts, in the correct order, to write efficiently and effectively.

Part One of *HOW TO WRITE* will show you how to organize for virtually any writing project. Part Two

will show you how to turn the material you've organized into a first draft. And Part Three will show
you how to turn that draft into a polished, ready-to-
go piece of writing.

*To use this book effectively, read it through once from
cover to cover. This will take roughly forty-five minutes.
You don't need to memorize anything at all. Your goal
is to become familiar with the three parts, and the key
steps within each part, that all together comprise the
process of writing. You want to begin thinking about
writing not as a mystical art form that depends utterly
on born talent or inspiration, but rather as a series of
decisions, steps, and techniques that you can master and
whose final result will be the clear, successful product
you want.*

Your real use of *HOW TO WRITE* will come when
you need to begin an actual project. Remember, this
is a handbook. So keep it handy. Use it to guide yourself
from start to finish through your own project. When
you begin an actual writing project, read through Part
One again and apply its decisions, steps, and techniques
to whatever it is you're writing. Only when you feel
that you've successfully organized for the job at hand
should you go on to Part Two. Likewise, only when
you've turned out an acceptable first draft, based on
the decisions, steps, and techniques outlined in Part
Two of *HOW TO WRITE*, should you go on to Part
Three.

Again, keep in mind that writing is a process. As
with any process, when you're just getting started its
various decisions, steps, and techniques always appear
to be more difficult and complicated than they really
are. And, as with any process, you can be sure that
this one will become much easier with experience.
Eventually, the various decisions, steps, and techniques
will become second nature. So don't be discouraged if
at first it all seems a bit difficult and complicated. After
a while it will all become natural — well, almost natural
— and writing itself will be much, much easier than
you ever imagined it could be.

Part One

ORGANIZING FOR THE JOB

Knowing how to organize for the job — for any job — is what separates the amateurs from the professionals. That's because organizing for a job is the least visible part of any process, and therefore the one that most amateurs don't know and, all too often, are not even aware exists. It's the part of a process that, when learned, usually leaves an amateur shaking his or her head ruefully while saying something like, "Oh, so that's how they do it."

On the other hand, a professional understands not only the need to organize properly for whatever job he or she plans to do, but also how to organize for that job. It makes no difference what the job is; you have to organize for it if you're going to do it properly. For instance, if you're going to paint a room you don't just run out to a hardware store, buy a brush and a bucket of paint, then run back home and start slapping the stuff on your walls. First you take down whatever pictures and curtains may be hanging, move your furniture to the center of the room, cover it up, and perhaps put masking tape around the window edges to keep paint from getting onto the glass. All this is organizing for the job, and if you've ever painted a room without organizing properly you know what a mess it can turn out to be. Likewise with baking a cake or bathing a baby; either you organize properly or you stumble your way through the process, wasting time and energy all the while and somehow never quite winding up how and where you want to be.

When you set out to write something — anything — organizing for the job is every bit as crucial as it is for any other process. Moreover, for reasons we simply cannot understand this part of the writing process generally receives the least amount of attention in schools and in writing textbooks. Some schools and textbooks don't teach organizing-for-the-job-of-writing at all. So don't be worried or upset if what follows in this section of *HOW TO WRITE* seems new and, at first, a bit odd. You'll master it quickly enough because it's really not that hard. In fact, it isn't hard at all. And when you have mastered the techniques of organizing-for-the-job-of-writing, don't be surprised to find yourself shaking *your* head ruefully and saying, "Oh, so that's how they do it."

As you will see in the steps that follow, organizing-for-the-job is primarily a thinking, list-making, and gathering-up process, during which you will need to:

> 1. *Choose your category,*
> 2. *Pick your points,*
> 3. *Collect your details.*

STEP ONE — Choosing Your Category:

The first step you need to take when you launch a writing project is so basic, and so obvious, that most people don't even realize that this step needs to be taken: You have to decide what it is you're going to write.

After all, every single piece of writing ever written fits into one or another category. There are literally dozens of categories, most of which you are already familiar with even though you may never actually have thought about it. For instance, there are press releases, articles for professional or trade journals, essays, book reviews, newspaper articles, advertisements, sales proposals, sales brochures, progress reports, reports of meetings, memos, letters of complaint, poems, novels, history textbooks, and so forth. To cite one rather obvious example, the item you are looking at this very moment is a "how-to" book, which is itself a very special and distinct category of writing.

It's important to recognize that all pieces of writing fit into one or another category, because each category has its own requirements, its own format, in short its own unique "look." Read through any ten sales proposals, and you will discover that no matter how different they are — no matter how different the products or services they are trying to sell — the similarities among the ten proposals are more striking than the differences. Each will refer to a product or service, each will articulate the advantages of this product or service to the proposed customer, and each will provide some basic information about the product or service such as cost, size, and so forth. Likewise, all book reviews — no matter what the book being reviewed, no matter what language the review is written in — give the book's title, author, and publisher. All describe the book under review, and all give some idea of the reviewer's opinion.

By deciding what it is you're going to write, you begin to focus on the requirements and format of your finished product. In a sense, it's like deciding what kind of a house you want to build; it makes it possible to think about the specific materials you're going to need — bricks, lumber, concrete, and so forth — and then about the design, so that in the end you get the finished product you want.

Sometimes the decision of what category of product to write is made for you. For instance, you might be a university student whose professor says: "I want you to read Mark Twain's novel *HUCKLEBERRY FINN* and write a review for our class one month from Thursday." Obviously, you will be writing a book review. If your favorite uncle has just sent you a birthday present and your mother hands you a pen and a piece of paper and tells you to sit down to express your appreciation, it's obvious that the item you'll be writing is a thank-you note. Or if you're an engineer with a California-based construction company whose boss asks you to fly to Chicago to see how the new shopping center is coming along, it's clear that what's wanted is a progress report.

But sometimes you will need to think through and make this first decision yourself. What if you buy a new television set, find it doesn't work properly, get no help from the store where you made your purchase, and decide to turn to the manufacturer for satisfaction? It only takes a minute's thought to realize that what you need to write is a letter of complaint. Sometimes it takes a little more thinking. Let's say you're a faculty member at a small college, attending an alumni dinner; the elderly gentleman sitting next to you says (rather grumpily) that in his day students owned typewriters but that none of the current students he talked with that afternoon own typewriters. He asks you why. You start to tell him — it's because today's students have switched over from typewriters to word processors, of course — when he interrupts and says that this development is so interesting that he'd like you to write it up for the next issue of the alumni bulletin. When you've had a chance to catch your breath and think for a moment, you'll realize that what you will need to write is a trend report.

As you can see, deciding what to write is not especially hard to do. It requires merely that you think ahead a little bit to consider the objective of whatever it is you will write. Is your objective to report, to inform, to suggest, to persuade, to stimulate action of one kind or another? What kind of writing product will best achieve this objective? You will be surprised at how easy it is to answer this last question, because in each case there is really only one category that will fit the bill. Determine your objective — that is, figure out the point of the exercise itself — and the correct category of writing product will fairly leap out at you.

Once you know just what sort of product you're going to write — either because someone has told you or because you made the decision yourself based on your judgment of what's needed — you are ready to take the second step: picking the points that will serve as the building blocks for your project.

STEP TWO — Picking Your Points:

Information is what makes a piece of writing go. After all, the purpose of writing something is to convey information. So it follows that information is the basic component of whatever you write. Indeed, information is to any piece of writing what cells are to a living creature, or what bricks and lumber are to a building.

It is what gives a piece of writing its shape, its thrust, its very character. Any piece of writing that includes all the necessary information in a sensible, comprehensible form will succeed, no matter what may be its other drawbacks or faults. Likewise, any piece of writing will fail that does not include the necessary information, no matter how eloquent its style and attractive its packaging. Always remember that when all is said and done, whatever you write will rise or fall on whether or not you've conveyed the information your reader needs.

In writing, information is divided into two parts: the point and the detail. A point is a piece of information that needs to be provided to a reader. A detail is the actual substance of that point. For example, in a book review you obviously need to tell your reader who wrote the book that you're reviewing. So that is a point you need to convey. The author's actual name is the detail. Or if you're writing a newspaper ad to sell your car, one point you'll need to provide is the mileage; the actual number is the detail. Consider that letter of complaint to the manufacturer of the television set that you recently bought and are unhappy with. Point: why you are unhappy. Detail: the remote-control gadget doesn't work.

In Step Two, your objective is merely to make a list of the points of information you're going to need for your piece of writing. Don't worry about collecting the details for these points; that's what you'll do in Step Three. For the moment, you need concentrate only on picking the points you're going to need.

The key to making a list of these necessary points lies in the category of product that you're writing. That's because each category has its own information requirements — its own list of points that must be included no matter what else is also thrown in. For example, consider this typical newspaper advertisement written by someone who is trying to rent out his house:

House for Rent — Three-story townhouse in the Cleve-

land Park section of Washington D.C. Two bedrooms, two bathrooms, dining room, den, living room with fireplace, modern kitchen, small garden, centrally air-conditioned. Price: $1,000 per month. Available on January 1. Call 233-1324.

Now consider the seven points of information this ad provides to its readers (for clarity's sake we've included the details, which are in italics, but for the moment you need focus only on the points):

1. The item for rent (*House for Rent*).
2. Description of the item (*three-story townhouse*).
3. Its location (*the Cleveland Park section of Washington D.C.*).
4. Its key features (*two bedrooms, two bathrooms, dining room, den, living room with fireplace, modern kitchen, small garden, centrally air conditioned.*)
5. The price (*$1,000 per month*).
6. Date of availability (*January 1*).
7. A way to get more information (*Call 233-1324*).

Obviously, the homeowner could have written an ad that provided many more points of information about the house — the type of heating system, whether or not there's a dishwasher, carpeting, and so forth. But the homeowner could not have written an ad that provided fewer points; the ones included in this ad are the absolute minimum any prospective renter would need to know simply to decide either to look elsewhere or be interested enough to seek more information.

Now read through this second example, which is a report of a meeting. Then we'll break down the report into a list of its key points, to show just how this report gives its intended reader all the information he or she is likely to need:

Report to: the Chairman
From: Vice President for Planning
Subject: Meeting of the Strategic Planning Committee

At this morning's meeting of the strategic planning committee, we decided to accelerate our growth for this year. More precisely, we decided to build not only the two factories in California we had already planned to build, but also to build a factory in Singapore.

Our decision to build this additional factory is based on your suggestion of last week that we give serious thought to a Singapore factory now, in light of our unexpected need to increase production to meet new orders, combined with the Government of Singapore's attractive financial offer made to you during your visit last month to that island country.

We estimate that the new factory will cost $3 million, and that construction could begin as early as April. If so, we believe production at this plant would begin no later than January of the following year.

At our meeting, we decided to seek bids from several construction firms, and to check with our company's major bankers to learn what sort of financial package they might offer to us. We expect preliminary responses from both the construction firms and the banks sometime next month.

Our decision to accelerate growth was not unanimous. Of our committee's five members — the vice presidents for planning, production, marketing, finance, and research — only three of us were originally in favor of the acceleration — planning, production, and marketing. The vice president for finance argued that construction of a factory in Singapore, now, would be too expensive; he felt the cost would diminish next year as the inflation rate falls. The vice president for research agreed with this, and added that in his judgment new production machinery would be available two years from now that would enable us to manufacture the same products at a lower cost; hence his conclusion that we would be wise to sit tight for the present.

After some discussion, the vice president for research withdrew his objection to the Singapore plant. Those of us who favored the project convinced him that the market for our product is so huge — now — that it would be a mistake to wait two years for more efficient equipment; by that time one of our competitors would have taken our customers.

The vice president for finance continues to oppose the project.

We plan to meet again next month here at head-quarters to review the situation and to assess our position.

Now, here's a breakdown of this report that lists its points. You can see how each one is absolutely nec-essary (once again, for clarity's sake we've included the details in italics):

1. The intended recipient (*the Chairman*).

2. The author (*Vice President for Planning*).

3. The subject (*Meeting of the Strategic Planning Committee*).

4. The key decision reached ("*to accelerate our growth for this year by building a factory in Singapore*").

5. The basis for this decision ("*your suggestion of last week . . . in light of our unexpected need to increase production . . . combined with the Government of Sing-apore's attractive offer . . .* ").

6. Relevant information about the decision:
— an estimate of the factory's cost (*$3 million*).
— an estimate of when construction could begin ("*as early as April*").

— an estimate of when production might start (*"no later than January of the following year"*).

— the next steps to be taken (*"we decided to seek bids from several construction firms, and to check with our company's major bankers . . . "*).

— the likely timetable (*"We expect preliminary responses . . . sometime next month"*).

— a report of differing opinions among those attending the meeting (*"Our decision to accelerate our growth was not unanimous . . . "*).

— a report of how these differing opinions were resolved (*"The vice president for research withdrew his objection . . . The vice president for finance continues to oppose the project"*).

7. A sense of what to expect next (*"We plan to meet again next month . . . to review the situation and assess our position"*).

In retrospect, it seems obvious that these points needed to be included — not merely in this report about this meeting, but in any report of any meeting. After all, the purpose of writing such a report is to let a reader know what went on, and only by providing these points can that be done. Could additional points have been provided? Of course. There's no limit to the number of points that could be provided, at least in theory. But the points that this report provides are the absolute minimum necessary to let a reader know what happened at a meeting which that reader did not attend. Obviously, no two meetings are the same. So of course the actual details will vary to reflect the unique substance and tone of each meeting. But the required points will always be the same in any report of any meeting.

To begin picking your points, first get your hands on a few examples of writing in the category you're working in. This is never hard to do, and it's always worth the effort. If you're writing a book review, collect a few reviews that others have written — it doesn't matter what book — and read them through. If you're placing an ad in a newspaper to sell your car, browse through a few newspapers to get a feel for what used-car ads look like and read like. You will be surprised at how easily you will be able to separate good examples from bad examples; how quickly you will reject examples that don't include points you know should be there, how easily you will be drawn toward examples precisely because they include the points that you — as a reader — feel a need to know.

Now, using a pen and paper or, if you prefer, working at your computer, start writing out the specific points you're going to need to produce your own piece of writing. Take your time; it's better to draw up a list that's too long rather than one that's too short because you left out some crucial points. And don't hesitate to include points whose details you don't as yet know; you can always get the details you need later, and indeed that's just what you will do. For now, just be sure that the list you make includes all the points you believe your reader or readers will need or want to know.

Quite a few professional writers use an imaginary question-and-answer technique to help zero in on the points their readers will need or want to know. It's a technique that at first will seem awkward and artificial, but one that after a while will become almost second nature. Here's the way to do it: Just for a moment, forget about the idea of writing anything at all. Imagine that you are sitting with the person who is the intended reader of whatever you are going to write. The two of you are having a conversation — not about just anything, but about the subject you are going to write about. Your imaginary reader asks questions; you answer them. Sometimes you know the answers; sometimes you don't. And as you run through this conversation in your mind, all the points that you will need to actually produce your piece of writing will start to emerge.

To illustrate this technique, let's return to that trend report we cooked up a few pages back; where the elderly alumnus asks you to write a piece for the alumni bulletin explaining that students no longer use typewriters because they've switched over to word processors. The imaginary conversation would go something like this:

"I hope you're not too upset that I asked you to write this trend report."

"The truth is, I've never actually done one before, and I'm not quite certain how to begin."

"Look at it from my point of view. The first thing I need to know is just what the trend itself really is."

"That's easy. I told you when we met: students are switching over from typewriters to word processors. But what else could you want to know?"

"Look, when you tell me that a trend is taking place, I can't help but wonder why it's taking place. There's always a reason."

"That's not hard either. Students are switching from typewriters to word processors because word processors are becoming affordable and because they're so much better than typewriters. Is this what you mean?"

"Precisely. But you see, each time you come forward with an interesting point it raises another question. Now I'm wondering how this trend is happening."

"How it's happening?"

"Of course. Are students going out and buying word processors? Are they being given these machines?"

"I don't know."

"I don't expect you to know. But I do expect you to find out and include your answer. That's not unreasonable, is it?"

"I suppose not. Would that be all you need?"

"You're my eyes and ears on this thing. I'm looking to you to tell me where this trend is going — what the future holds."

"I'm embarrassed to say this, but again I don't know."

"And again, I say that I don't expect you to know. I expect you to find out and to tell me."

"Okay. I'll get going on these points. But is there anything else you're looking for in this trend report?"

"Yes. Just one more thing. I'd like your own personal judgment about the trend. What do you think about it?

*Is it a good trend? A bad one? Is it important? Do you
see what I'm driving at?"*

*"Yes. I think so. You want to know what the trend
is, why it's happening, how it's happening, where it's
going, and what I think of it all. These are the points
you need me to cover. Have I got it now?"*

"Oh yes. Indeed you do."

Relax. Enjoy yourself. If you don't like the way you
handled yourself during the imaginary conversation —
do it again. And this time go a bit more slowly. Think
through your answers; experiment with them a bit.
Don't be embarrassed; this is all happening in your
mind, and no one except you will ever know about it.
Haven't you ever wished for a second chance to say
all the clever and witty things you didn't say when you
should have? Well, now's your chance. After all, you
get to make up the questions as well as the answers,
so do it your way. Play around with your words and
your ideas until you begin to feel you've got a grip on
things.

And never, never lose sight of what you started out
to do. Namely, to make a list of those points you will
absolutely, positively need to satisfy the requirements
of the particular category into which your piece of
writing falls; the points that you, as a reader, would
need or want to know if someone else were writing this
piece for you.

Since this step requires more thinking than actual
writing, there's no need to remain glued to your chair.
Quite a few professional writers spend a hefty chunk
of their time walking around, jogging, grocery shopping, washing their cars, or whatever. As long as you
are not actually putting words on paper or on a computer screen, you can do anything you want so long as
you are able to think at the same time. Indeed, sometimes it helps a lot to get away from the table or desk.
Nobody who reads your finished product will have the
slightest idea how you spent your time during its production. Nobody will care, either. Keep in mind that
"writing" is a step-by-step process, in which quite a
few of the steps require no actual writing at all.

In any case, however you choose to do it you must eventually turn out a list of the various points you're going to need. The list should be simple, direct, and brief enough to fit easily on one side of a single sheet of paper. Once again using our trend report as an example, a list of point would look like this:

Trend Report

1. What the trend is

2. Why the trend is taking place

3. How the trend is happening

4. Where the trend is going

5. What I (the writer) think of it all

Read through the list once or twice. Make certain that you're comfortable with it. If not, go ahead and revise the list. Focus only on picking the points you're going to need for whatever category of writing you've chosen. Don't spend your time or energy worrying about anything except picking the right points.

And when you've made a list of the key points that your piece of writing must include — stop. Now you are ready for the next step, which is to go out and collect the details you haven't yet got.

STEP THREE — *Collecting Your Details:*

The single greatest cause of panic-stricken paralysis among writers is neither lack of confidence nor lack of inspiration. Rather, it is lack of a specific detail the writer needs at a particular moment to flesh out a point he or she knows must be made, combined with a stubborn refusal to face up to the problem and to treat it with the only remedy that works: namely, going out and collecting that detail.

To grasp the importance of this go-out-and-get-what-

you-need business, imagine for a moment that you are
in your kitchen, preparing a dinner party for some
friends. Now, a dinner party is a category of meal, and
just like a category of writing it has its own requirements: something to start, a main course, a dessert.
Let's say your menu will be soup, followed by roast
beef with potatoes and carrots, then vanilla ice cream
with chocolate sauce for dessert. It's 5 p.m. and your
guests are due to arrive at eight o'clock. You suddenly
realize that, although you've been grocery shopping
twice for this dinner party, you have somehow forgotten
to buy the roast. Alas, there are no plausible substitutes
in the freezer — no lamb chops, no steaks, no hamburger. Clearly, you have two ways to go: make do
without the roast, or scramble out to the supermarket.
You really haven't got much choice, have you? Unless
you want to take a chance that your guests are total
idiots and won't notice that the main course is missing.
Obviously, you decide to dash out to the supermarket
despite the late hour and the inconvenience.

Now imagine that the item you forgot to buy during
your shopping expeditions is the chocolate sauce. Since
vanilla ice cream tastes delicious all by iteslf (and since
no one will ever know you'd planned to serve chocolate
sauce, unless you tell them), you say to heck with it.
You didn't want the extra calories, anyway.

What ingredients are to a meal, details are to a piece
of writing. Some are more important than others. Some
are expendable if the effort required to get them is too
great. Others require the effort at whatever cost. Moreover, some of the crucial ones aren't obviously crucial
as is, say, a main-course roast to a dinner party. What
if you hadn't bothered to buy salt? Or sugar and cream
for the coffee? It can be such a small ingredient — or
detail — that makes the difference between smooth
sailing and rough going, between success and failure.

Collecting details for a piece of writing is very much
like grocery shopping for a dinner party. You start by
making a list of the requirements for the category
you've chosen — which is what you did in Step Two.
Then you check off those items for which the details

(the ingredients, as it were) are already on hand. And, finally, you go out to get whatever you need but haven't yet got. If in the end you discover that you forgot a detail — like forgetting an ingredient when you're shopping, it happens to everyone now and then — you then must decide whether it's crucial or merely desirable. If it's crucial, you scramble out to get it whatever the cost or inconvenience. If it's merely desirable, you use your best judgment.

These are the key principles of collecting details for any piece of writing:

— Anticipate
— Be energetic
— Be dogged
— Be imaginative

Anticipate: Keep in mind that the writing process begins when the need arises to write something; not when you finally sit down to turn out a first draft. The sooner you begin to collect the details you're going to need, the better off you'll be; the less time and effort you'll need to devote to collection and, therefore, the more time and effort you can pour into later phases of the writing process.

By anticipating the details you're going to need, you give yourself a head start on collecting them. Let's say you show up one evening at your child's school for a meeting of the parent-teacher association; the PTA president takes you aside, tells you that the parent who usually writes up the meeting-report for the PTA bulletin has called in sick, and asks you to write the report and have it ready for printing and distribution the next day. Now, it's likely that the meeting will last for roughly one hour, and that you'll be working late into the night to complete your report. It's also likely that the participants in the meeting will be hard to find after the meeting ends — or, worse, fast asleep. By anticipating what details you're going to need, you can collect them before the meeting breaks up. For example, you're obviously going to need the names and school-or-PTA titles of key participants. No big deal; just be sure to ask someone — and to write down his or her answers — either just before the meeting starts or just after it ends. If during the course of the meeting somebody mentions "the Bradley project" — which you have never heard of before — make sure to grab that person before he or she escapes to get a brief explanation.

Never be embarrassed to tell people what you're doing and to ask them for help. How do you actually do this? You do it the easy way; you just go up to them and ask: "Excuse me, but my name is So-and-So and I've been asked to write up a report on this meeting. Would you be kind enough to tell me the correct spelling of your name and your precise title? Thanks so much." Don't worry; it almost always works. Most people are very nice and very pleasant. Or, if someone says something that you just don't grasp, get hold of that individual after the meeting, tell him or her your problem, and ask for some help. You'll get it. And don't be embarrassed to admit that you're still not sure you understand; just say that you'll be writing your report during the evening, and ask for a telephone number where the person can be reached. You'll get the number — and with gratitude to boot. Intelligent people would rather you reported what they said accurately, even if it causes them some minor inconvenience.

Your ability to anticipate the details you're going to need, and thus your ability to efficiently collect them as you move along, will grow dramatically as you become familiar and comfortable with the writing process. You'll be surprised at how easy it becomes to spot necessary details as, so to speak, you roll your grocery cart down the aisle. And when you sit down to actually write out that list of points you're going to need, you'll find that you already have in hand more and more of the details too.

Be Energetic: Keep in mind that there's a lot more to "writing" than running your pencil across paper or tapping away on your computer keyboard. You must devote much of your effort to collecting the material you will need to choose your words and write your sentences. And this is more of a physical than a mental chore. So don't be lazy. If there's a detail you know you're going to need — go get it. For instance, if you are writing a review of a new restaurant your readers will need to know if the place accepts telephone reservations. There's just one way to find out, and that's by asking the owner or manager. So ask. In a trip-report on a visit to the Empire State Building, you must assume your reader already knows that the building is tall. What you must tell your reader is how tall. So reach across to your almanac or encyclopedia — or trot off to the nearest library — and look it up.

Or if you're a real estate agent writing a sales brochure for a farm that's just come onto the market, don't settle for saying that the place has "several hundred" acres. Your readers will want to know precisely how many acres there are. What's that? You say you forgot to ask the owner when you toured the place? Big deal; we all goof up from time to time. Go back and ask him, or simply call him up. And if by some odd chance he doesn't know the answer to your question, hire a surveyor to measure the place. Or, if you're trying to convince your boss to rent office space in one building or another, keep in mind that he'll need to know precisely how the rents compare with each other. Get the numbers and put them in your memo. (And if driving time from the office to the airport is important, get in your car and make the comparison yourself; there's nothing like first-hand research to give your report credibility and weight.)

Get out of your chair. Use a telephone, use your feet, jump in your car or saddle up your horse. Look it up, check it out, pin it down. You will more than make up for lost time when you finally sit down to write your first draft. The biggest time-waster of all is sitting down and becoming paralyzed because you didn't spend the energy to gather up the details you knew darn well you were going to need.

Be Dogged: Collecting details can be fun. Indeed, for some writers this is far and away the most enjoyable phase of the entire process. But collecting details can also be a ferocious pain in the neck. You slug your way through rush-hour traffic to the library — and discover when you get inside that the volume of the encyclopedia you need is missing. Or that some thoughtless idiot has ripped out the page of the almanac that would have given you the precise height and number of stories of the Empire State Building. Or you telephone the individual who has the detail you need, only to be told that the blinking so-and-so has just left the country to go hiking in the Himalayas and won't be back for six weeks at least. No, you are told by his coolly efficient (and utterly useless) secretary, there is no one else in the office who can help you.

Don't be discouraged. And for heaven's sake, don't give up too easily. Very often the difference between a successful piece of writing and a failure is not the literary quality of the prose or even the skill of its organization, but rather the doggedness of its research. When you come right down to it, there are really very few details that can't be found; mostly it's a question of time and effort.

The decision of how hard to work for a needed detail — how much time and effort to devote — is always a matter of judgment. Human nature being what it is — more precisely, most of us being more or less on the lazy side — the tendency is always to give up when the going gets rough. Good writers learn to be just a bit more dogged. When they can't get a necessary detail the easy way, they do it the hard way. This means a bit more time and effort, such as going to another library, or looking in two or three reference books, or making a few more telephone calls, or whatever. You'll be amazed at how often just a little bit of extra time and effort pays off in the end.

Keep in mind that when you write for someone — no matter what you write; no matter who you write it for — you become your reader's eyes, ears, legs, and even intellect. In a very real sense, you are acting as an extension of your reader. So do the kind of job you would want someone else to do for you.

Be Imaginative: Few things do more for a piece of writing than newly discovered details, or well known details described in wholly new and interesting ways. If you're writing a letter to a business executive, trying to convince him to locate his new factory in your town, think how persuasive it would be if you could write that six of his ten largest customers were headquartered within a radius of 50 miles, or that each year the local college graduates roughly 100 students with precisely the skills his workforce would require. Or if you're working with a church group that's trying to raise money to help feed hungry children in Africa, and you've been asked to write a letter soliciting donations from members of the congregation, rather than just ask for money think of how much more effective it is to point out that $5 would keep a child alive for nearly two weeks, and that $20 would keep an entire family from starving for that period. These are the sorts of details that carry weight; that make a difference to the reader. It's your job as a writer to go beyond the obvious details, and to think up new ones that will enlighten your reader and take him or her in the direction you want to go.

Discovering new details often is just a matter of asking questions. You casually ask the owner of the house for whom you're writing a sales brochure whether he's the original owner — and discover that he bought the place from a famous actor. Now that's worth mentioning in the sales brochure. Or when you ask the owner of the restaurant you're reviewing how he happened to open the place, he matter-of-factly tells you he used to be chief chef at the White House, but decided to leave Washington because the climate there was bad for his daughter's allergies. Wow! Obviously, you don't get lucky every time. But you'd be surprised how often you come up with something interesting —

and therefore useful — when you actively look for it; when you open your eyes and your energies to whatever may be available.

Always keep an eye open for imaginative ways to present details that are already well known. If you're trying to describe how many bars of chocolate a candy manufacturer has sold, don't just give the number; give your reader a visual idea of how many bars that really is: "The company has sold 55 million chocolate bars — enough bars to fill up Yankee Stadium from home plate to the top row of the bleachers." Or, if for a paper on the Common Market's economic problems you were trying to describe the amount of surplus butter in Western Europe — what economists call the "butter mountain" — why not point out that this "mountain" is so huge that if spread over Vienna it would cover the entire city to a depth of six inches. All you need to come up with imaginative ways to present your details is the idea itself; a pocket calculator helps.

Don't be afraid to try something different. Reach for a new detail, or a new way to describe a well-known detail. You will enlighten your reader and, more importantly, hold your reader's interest. And by doing so you will guide your reader in the direction you have chosen to go.

To illustrate these principles of collecting details, let us return again to that trend report whose points we picked back in Step Two. And let's put ourselves in the writer's position. The trick will be to take each point in turn, and to pour on whatever effort is required to get the necessary information. Our objective is a list made up of the points and, below each point, its particular details. Remember, this list will be for our own use — no one else will ever see it. So we don't need to worry about format, neatness, or style. We just need to make certain that the list meets our need for information.

To refresh your memory, we decided that the points of a trend report are:

1. What the trend is
2. Why the trend is taking place
3. How the trend is happening
4. Where the trend is going
5. What I (the writer) think of it all

In this particular example, we've got a leg up because we already know the details for the first point: we know what the trend is, namely that students are switching over from typewriters to word processors. Indeed, it was the casual mention of this trend that triggered the need to write. Since we already have this ingredient on hand, so to speak, we can move along to the second point. To learn why the trend is taking place, we would go talk with students who themselves have made the switchover. We would ask them why they did it, then write down their answers. We might also ask members of the college staff what they know about the trend. As to how the trend is happening, again we would ask the students and college staff. But in addition, it wouldn't hurt to stop by a local computer store and ask the store manager for his point of view. For details on where the trend is going, we would ask the very same people. But to broaden our understanding, we would also stop by the library, look up "word processing" in the catalog, flip through some magazines, and ask the librarian for any material that might be available on the subject of students using word processors. For the last point — our own evaluation of the trend — we would rely again on all these sources, and perhaps also on the judgments of some "experts" we've managed to locate, for example in the computer-sciences faculty of the college. We would distill their thinking into our own personal point of view.

We end up with a list which looks like this:

1. What the trend is

Students are switching over from typewriters to word processors.

2. Why the trend is taking place

The trend is happening because word processors are better than typewriters ... easier to use, with far more capabilities. Also word processors are becoming more affordable.

3. How the trend is happening

Students are buying their own word processors ... The college is making available a list of "acceptable" models that are compatible with the college's own equipment ... Students loans are available for the purchase of word processors ... College is offering a course to students who buy word processors to show them how to use the equipment ... professors are encouraging the use of word processors by allowing students to send in their homework assignments electronically to their professors, who grade these assignments by reading them on their own terminals and by sending their comments directly to the students through their own terminals.

4. Where the trend is going

Heading for a time when all students at the college will be using word processors ... They will use them to prepare assignments, to search through data banks for information, to transmit homework assignments to professors ... perhaps even to communicate with one another. In a few year's time, word processors will be required for all students.

5. What I (the writer) think of it all

Since word processors are more efficient than typewriters, it follows that students who use word processors will become more efficient ... .Of course, word processors are not the answer to everything ... not a substitute for

*thinking, reading, working. These machines are a tool,
no more no less. On balance the trend is a good one.*

When we've made our list, we'll read through it once
or twice. We'll do it carefully, taking a few extra minutes not only to read but to think. We might even get
up to take a walk or get a drink of water. Our focus
at this point is on substance rather than style. We just
need to be certain that the details we've collected explain the points that we've picked. Again, we won't
worry about format, neatness, or style. This list is for
our own use, and no one but us will ever see it. If we
can see some way to improve or expand what we've
written, we'll go ahead and make the change. If it looks
all right, we'll leave it alone.

Don't be surprised — or discouraged — if all this
thinking, choosing, collection, and list-making activity
that we've outlined here in Part One of *HOW TO
WRITE* seems a bit awkward or difficult at first. As
we said at the outset, organizing-for-the-job is far and
away the most "invisible" part of the writing process.
Moreover, for reasons we cannot understand it's the
part that schools and universities rarely if ever teach.
Little wonder, then, that so many people have trouble
writing; they're not taught the first part of the process
and are somehow expected to start with the second
part and go from there — which simply can't be done.
If it takes you a while to decide what it is you're going
to write, to make a list of necessary points, and then
to gather up your details — don't worry about it. The
time you spend learning to master these steps and techniques will serve you well. Just remember the Meyers'
first (and only) law of writing: any piece of writing that
conveys the necessary information in some reasonable
and coherent order will succeed no matter what its
other flaws and drawbacks.

And when at last you've decided what it is you're
going to write, made your list of necessary points for
this particular category of writing, and collected all
your details, you have completed the vital, "invisible"
part of the writing process that all professionals know
makes the difference between failure and success. In-

deed, after completing this part of the process you have actually got in hand everything you need to begin turning out your first draft. In Part Two we'll show you how to put it all together.

Part Two

TURNING OUT
A FIRST DRAFT

Turning out a first draft is far and away the most decisive part of the writing process. For this is when you begin to commit yourself to a specific course of action; to a detailed and precise architecture of the finished product.

To be sure, you can write second drafts, third drafts, fourth drafts — even tenth drafts if you want to. And, once you are familiar with the skills and techniques of draft-polishing, you will have little difficulty making each successive draft better than the one before. But no matter how many drafts you write, it's the first draft that always has the biggest influence on your finished product. The others are merely modifications and improvements of the original, first-draft architecture. In this sense, turning out a first draft is a bit like constructing a building; once you've put up the walls and laid down the roof, whatever changes you make are at best important modifications. You can improve the building — often dramatically and with surprisingly little effort — but not change its architecture in any fundamental way. You can make a telephone booth a better telephone booth, a hamburger stand a better hamburger stand, and a factory a better factory. But you can not really turn a telephone booth into a hamburger stand, or a hamburger stand into a factory, or a factory into a telephone booth.

In other words, shortcomings and mistakes in the *execution* of a first draft can be overcome and repaired; that's precisely what second, third, fourth, even tenth drafts are for. But if you make an *architectural* mistake in the first draft — that is, if you build the wrong thing, however well you build it — you're more or less stuck. Why can't you just tear up the entire mess and start over again? In theory, you can. You may even be able to do it in practice. But as a general rule, by the time you've written out a first draft you've expended too much time and intellectual energy simply to throw out what you've done and start all over again from scratch. At this point, you'll be scrambling furiously to make the best of what you've got, either because you've run short of time or because you've burned up too much intellectual energy. Again, you can improve a first draft, often dramatically and with surprisingly little effort. So flaws and shortcomings in the execution are nothing at all to worry about. At this point, you need be concerned only with choosing the right architecture. That is your primary objective in turning out a first draft.

As you will see in the steps that follow, turning out a first draft is primarily a focusing, sketching-out, and construction process, during which you will need to:

> *1. Figure out your theme,*
> *2. Make your outline,*
> *3. Write your draft.*

STEP ONE — Figuring Out Your Theme:

Every piece of writing has a theme. It's always in there somewhere. The difference between successful pieces of writing and unsuccessful pieces is this: in successful ones the theme is written out so clearly that the reader has no trouble grasping it, while in unsuccessful pieces of writing the theme is so obscure, so buried and scattered throughout the text, that either it can't be grasped at all by the reader or the effort required to grasp it is more than any reader can be expected to make. It's the difference between showing someone a building or showing someone a pile of wood, bricks, nails and mortar and asking him or her to imagine how the building would look if only you had taken the trouble to put it all together.

Think of it this way: since the point of any piece of writing is to communicate ideas and information, to succeed you must do the reader's work — that is to say, his thinking — for him. You must show him what you mean, not throw a bunch of words, sentences, and paragraphs at him and hope the poor devil will have the time, skill and inclination to figure it out for himself. That's why the first step in turning out a first draft is for you to figure out your own theme so that you can put it right up front, literally at the very top of your piece of writing. In this way — and only in this way — can you be sure that your reader will see clearly what you mean.

A theme captures in just a few words or sentences — in other words, a theme summarizes — what it is you want to say about the subject at hand. Thus it is not the same thing as the subject itself. It is more like the explanation of the subject; it answers the question, "Well, what about it?". Let's say you get a telephone call from a friend who is president of the local Professional Women's Association. She tells you that the group holds a luncheon every other Wednesday, and she invites you to be their guest at the next session and to deliver a short talk on the subject of "Working Mothers." You accept the invitation (you hate speaking in public, but you owe her a favor so you can't say no) and now you sit down to write your speech. Here are just a few of the possible themes a speech on the subject of "Working Mothers" might have:

Working mothers have gone from a small if interesting phenomenon to a major segment of today's work force. In doing so, this has fundamentally changed not only our country's work force, but our family lifestyles. As more and more mothers take jobs — and as more and more women continue working after starting families — these changes will become more profound and more lasting.

— With this as your theme, you would probably go on to provide the statistical evidence to show just how rapidly the number of working mothers has grown. You would explain how family lifestyles have changed now that so many mothers are holding jobs, and you would probably project what future changes are likely as still more mothers join the work force. No doubt you would offer your own opinion of these developments. In effect what you're writing here, for oral delivery as a speech, is a trend report.

Now that the majority of mothers work, the time has come for a program of action to bring business practices and regulations into line with reality. At present our system, designed for an age when women with children stayed home, fails utterly to take the needs of working mothers into account. This is both unfair and counter-productive.

— With this as your theme, you would go on to outline why and how the present system is unfair to working mothers. Then you would outline a series of reforms designed to modernize business practices and regulations, for example a program to enable flexible working hours for women with children, more liberal maternity-leave benefits, and expanded tax deductions for day-care expenditures. You would explain how these changes would be more fair, and how they would enable working mothers, and thus our country's economy, to become more productive. In effect what you're writing here, again for oral delivery as a speech, is a course-of-action memo.

I'm sick and tired of hearing working mothers complain about their problems. Ironically, the complaining doesn't come from all those women who work because their families need the money they earn to eat. The complaining comes from those affluent, upwardly-mobile women who work not because they must, but because they want to; because staying at home with their children doesn't offer enough satisfaction for them. Of course these women have every right to work, but that doesn't mean society must change to accommodate their efforts to have their cake and eat it, too. Mothers who choose to stay at home with young children also "work" — hard — and it's time we devoted a bit more attention to their problems and needs.

— With this as your theme, you would go on to sharply criticize working mothers who are part of the current movement to change business practices and regulations to accommodate their own unique needs. You would explain why you don't share their view, and why you believe acceptance of their program would be detrimental. You would offer a strong defense of mothers who choose to stay at home with their children, and you might go on to highlight some of their unique needs and perhaps offer some suggestions for how to ease their burdens. In effect what you would be writing here, for oral delivery as a speech, is a personal-point-of-view paper. (And given the forum for which this paper/speech is intended, you might also be writing your obituary. But that's another matter.)

As you can see, knowing what the subject is tells you very little about the theme. Why? Because you can write your piece to make it go in virtually any direction. But the one thing that you cannot do is expect your reader to figure out, by him- or herself, the direction in which you have chosen to go. You — the writer — have got to do this for your reader by clearly articulating your own theme. Here's another set of theme examples, this time of newspaper editorial-page articles on the complex and always controversial subject of "US-Soviet Relations":

US-Soviet relations have skidded to their worst level in twenty years. This has occurred because the Soviet Union has embarked on a series of dangerous activities designed to undermine the West and weaken the will of Western countries to arm themselves against further Soviet aggression. It is important that the people and leaders of Western countries resist the temptation to give in to Soviet demands in an effort to ease tensions. Doing so would damage our own national-security interests, and only encourage the Soviets to put more pressure on us to make additional concessions.

— An editorial with this as its theme would focus on a listing of recent Soviet activities of which the writer disapproves, followed by an explanation of why giving

in to Soviet demands would be foolhardy and dangerous
for the West.

On the other hand, with the very same subject —
US-Soviet relations — the theme could be this:

*US-Soviet relations can be improved, dramatically
and quickly, if only the US would agree to open a series
of arms-control negotiations based on the Soviet Union's
latest proposal. It's hard to understand why Washington
is refusing to take the new Soviet proposal seriously. To
be sure, the Soviet proposal isn't perfect. But it does
contain some new elements, and Washington's out-of-
hand dismissal of the proposal as "the same old stuff;
nothing new" is wholly unjustified. Moreover, it is so
important to improve US-Soviet relations that too much
fussing over details is dangerous.*

— An editorial with this as its theme would develop
by listing the key points of the new Soviet proposal,
followed by an analysis of these points and an explanation of why the proposal should be taken seriously
by Washington. The editorial might go on to suggest
an approach to negotiating a new arms-control agree-
ment based on the Soviet proposal that would be acceptable to US national interests.

Or even this could be the theme of an editorial on
US-Soviet relations:

*The state of US-Soviet relations is irrelevant. It mat-
ters only to a few politicians and diplomats who care
about their own selfish interests and not at all about
mankind itself. What really matters to people are issues
close to their own daily lives, such as the quality of the
air we breathe, of the water we drink, and in general
our personal environments. If only the leaders of the US
and the Soviet Union would pay more attention to or-
dinary people, there wouldn't be so much trouble and*

tension between the so-called superpowers. Both sides therefore should destroy their weapons so everyone could live in peace with no more danger of war.

— An editorial with this as its theme would develop into a general attack on politicians and on politics itself. It would likely be a plea for peace that urges more emphasis on the common bonds among people throughout the world and less emphasis on the nuts and bolts of national defense policies.

It's obvious that figuring out your theme is an especially critical step. The good news is that it isn't very hard to do. You just have to be careful. Keep in mind that your goal is to come up with a few short sentences that capture precisely whatever it is you mean. The best way to start is with the list of points that you picked back in Part One. Look at your subject — which of course is the very first point on your list — and then ask yourself the key question: "Well, what about this subject? What's my objective?" Are you trying to talk your reader into something? Or out of something? Are you trying to persuade, to be helpful, merely to convey information, to trigger some specific course of action, or to expound your own personal point of view?

If the theme doesn't leap out at you — and it rarely does — then read through the various details that you collected to see if they don't provide a clue. They often do. And if the theme still hasn't leapt out at you, try doing what you did in Part One, when you organized for the job. That is, settle down, relax, and have yourself an imaginary conversation with whomever is the intended reader of whatever it is you're planning to write. Here's the imaginary conversation that we had with you, just before we sat down to write the first draft of this very book you're reading now:

"So tell me, what sort of a piece are you writing?"
"It's a book. More precisely, it's a how-to book designed to show people how to write."

"How very interesting. Tell me, what's your theme?"

"Well, er, you see, what we're trying to do is, um, to —"

"Don't panic. We'll work it out. Tell me, have you got some unique approach to the subject?"

"Sure we do. You see, everybody thinks that writing is some sort of mysterious art; a sort of talent that either you have or you don't."

"But that's true, isn't it?"

"No. It isn't true at all. Writing is just a process — like cooking, or carpentry, or cleaning a house. Of course, not everyone can be a great cook, or a great carpenter, or a great house-cleaner. But anybody can learn the process, and with a bit of practice do a fairly decent job."

"I see. So this is your approach?"

"Yes, I suppose it is."

"But what exactly is this process, as you call it? Can you articulate it for me?"

"This isn't the time to go into too much detail. But in general it works like this: First, you organize for the job. Then you turn out a first draft. Then you polish that draft until you've got a decent, effective finished product. As we say, you do all this through a series of little steps taken in the proper sequence."

"It sounds like we're beginning to focus on a theme. If I understand you correctly, it runs like this: Writing well requires neither art nor talent. That's because writing is a process like any other. Thus it can be learned. In essence, there are three parts to the writing process, with each part containing a number of specific steps. The three parts are organizing for the job, turning out a first draft, and polishing the draft into an effective, finished product."

"Hey, it sounds like we've figured out the theme."

"I believe we have."

Don't be surprised if it takes a fair amount of time and effort to figure out your theme. And don't be discouraged, either. And above all, don't give up. In the history of writing, there has never been a piece of

writing that didn't have a theme that could be artic-
ulated in a few, clearly written sentences. And there
never will be such a piece. It's just that some themes
are a bit harder than others to work out.

So take your time. Remember, there's no rule which
requires you to sit at your desk, or to stare at your
computer while the cursor blinks away in the upper
left-hand corner of a blank screen, while you think
things out. Do whatever is most comfortable for you.
If you need to sit down and put words on paper, or
tap them onto your computer screen — go right ahead.
But don't be reluctant to get up and walk around, or
jog, or wash the dishes, or whatever. As we said earlier,
quite a few professional writers find that physical activity of one sort or another helps them to think clearly
— and this is one step in the writing process where
clear thinking is essential.

Now let's return yet another time to that trend report
we launched back in Part One. Having chosen our
category, picked our points, and collected our details,
we need to figure out our theme. Since it isn't leaping
out at us — no big deal; as we said, themes rarely do
— it's time for another imaginary conversation with
our intended reader:

"Hello again. How's your project coming along?"

*"Not so well, I'm afraid. I'm having a bit of trouble
figuring out my theme."*

*"Well, that happens. Tell me, what did you find out
when you were out there collecting all your details? What
did you learn?"*

"I've got my list, but —"

*"Then look at it. Study it. What does it tell you? Try
to distill the meaning of what you found out. Stand back
from it a bit. That usually helps."*

*"Let me think for a moment. I learned that students
at our college are in the midst of a switchover, from
typewriters to word processors. The switchover is taking
place because word processors are better, easier to use,
and affordable. Is this what you mean?"*

"It's precisely what I mean. Just keep going."

*"Okay. Students are making the trend happen by
buying their own machines, and the college is helping
with advice, financing, and with instruction courses.
Moreover, the college is encouraging the trend by allowing students to use word processors for more and more
assignments. We're heading for a time when all students
will be using word processors. How am I doing?"*

"Beautifully. What else?"

*"Just my own view of it, which is that on balance the
trend is a good one."*

"Why is that?"

"Why?"

*"Yes, why. Look, I can read anything you write, but
I can't read your mind. When you make a judgment,
you've got to give me, in writing, some explanation of
why you hold that point of view. Now, you were saying
that on balance the trend is a good one?"*

*"Yes, that's right. Students who use word processors
are more efficient. That's always good. Have I got it
now?"*

*"If you think about it for a moment, you'll realize
that you've figured out your theme. Just catch your
breath and spell it out in one burst."*

*"Okay, here goes. Students at our college are in the
midst of a switchover, from typewriters to word processors. The switchover is taking place because word processors are better, easier to use, and affordable. Students
are making the trend happen by buying their own machines, and the college is helping. Moreover, the college
is encouraging the trend. We're heading for a time when
all students will be using word processors. On balance,
the trend is a good one. Is that my theme?"*

"It certainly is."

Keep in mind that writing takes a certain tenacity.
Things don't always work out right the first time; you
make a mistake and wind up with a bit of a mess, or
realize you missed something along the way. There's
nothing to do but shrug off the mistakes, or clean up
the mess, or go back over the part to add something
you realize you missed the first time. In short, there's

nothing to do but to try again. So if you don't like the way that your imaginary conversation with your intended reader works out, have a second or even a third imaginary conversation. Likewise with whatever you write down on paper or tap out on your computer. Nobody will ever see the material you toss out, so don't be embarrassed to try something even if it turns out to be a flop. Work out as many variations as you need until you get the theme that you want.

And how will you know when you've got the theme that you want? You're not going to like the answer to this one: The answer is, you can't be sure you've got the "right" theme. At least, you can't be sure just yet. You need to go on a bit, at least to the next step. For it is only as you work your way through the next step — which is making an outline — that you can determine for sure whether the theme you've just worked out is the "right" one for the piece you're writing.

STEP TWO — Making an Outline:

An outline serves two key purposes. First, an outline serves as a check — a test — on what you've done up to now. Just like the steel girders of a skyscraper, a writing outline suggests the shape and size of the product-to-be. If it looks like what you had in mind — fine. You keep going. But if the outline suggests a product-to-be that isn't what you want or need — boy, will it ever be visible to you. In other words, if you're on the right track an outline will make this clear. But if in fact you've made an important error of judgment along the way and wound up with the "wrong" theme — wrong, that is, for the piece you want to write — this is when you'll catch it. And you will be able to make the necessary changes before you've strayed too far off course and burned up too much time and energy to turn back.

Second, an outline acts as a skeleton for the draft itself. For when you've gotten your outline right it serves — again, like the steel girders of a skyscraper

— as a visible, sturdy frame that you can beef up and flesh out until it becomes a semi-finished and then a finished product.

To make your outline, begin by writing out a title at the top of the page. You needn't worry about whether it's an especially wonderful title; it's for your own use, and you'll have plenty of time to come up with a better title later on. For now, just put down the first title that pops into your head. (You'll be surprised at how often the first title that pops into your head turns out to be the best one.) Now write out your theme below the title. This will amount to a fairly solid paragraph. Then write out the points you've picked along with the details that will flesh out these points. In doing so, this time combine the points and the details, as appropriate, so that what you write appears in complete, understandable sentences. For convenience's sake, continue to number the points.

This theme-points-details list will work for you as an outline by serving as a skeleton and thus illuminating what your finished product will look like. Of course, if you don't like the way your product is going to look, now's your chance to fix it. In many cases, you will be able to do this simply by shifting around or modifying the numbered points. But if this shifting and modifying doesn't do the trick, you may be certain that the problem lies with the theme you've developed. If so, this is when you "stop the presses" to go back and develop the theme that's right for your piece of writing.

Returning once again to our trend report, here's what the outline would look like:

The Switchover to Word Processors

Students at our college are in the midst of a switchover, from typewriters to word processors. The switchover is taking place because word processors are better, easier to use, and affordable. Students are making the trend happen by buying their own machines, and the college is helping. Moreover, the college is encouraging the trend.

We're heading for a time when all students will be using word processors. On balance, the trend is a good one.

1. Students are switching over from typewriters to word processors.

2. Students are making the trend happen by buying their own word processors. The college is helping by providing a list of "acceptable" models, by offering loans, and instruction courses. Professors are encouraging the trend.

3. The trend is taking place because word processors are better than typewriters. They are easier to use, have more capabilities, and are becoming more affordable.

4. As for where the trend is going, we're heading for a time when all students at the college will be using word processors. In a few years, use of these machines will be required.

5. As for my own judgment, it's clear that students who use word processors will be more efficient. To be sure, these machines are no more than a tool. They are not a substitute for thinking, reading, working. But on balance I believe the trend is a good one.

Now let's read through the outline once or twice. How does it look? Surely you can see what the first draft based on this outline would be like. Is this the product we have in mind to write? Will it serve our purpose? Will it make sense to our reader? Are we comfortable with it? Let's not worry about little details and small points, but is anything important missing? No? Good. Whoops — hang on a minute! Should we include a section that outlines the growing use of computers on campus for purposes other than word processing, for example in the college administrative office? We could slip in a section like this after the current Section 4. Let's think for a moment. No doubt such a section would be accurate and interesting. But is it necessary? Well, necessary is putting it a bit too strongly. So it's a judgment call. We've been prudent to consider adding in the section, but in this case let's give ourselves a break and leave it out after all.

Now, is everything in the best possible order? What's that? You'd rather we tell our reader why students are making the trend happen before telling him how the trend is happening? Okay; there's no law which requires the "how" to come before the "why" of a trend report. Just reverse points 2 and 3. Is that better? Fine. Now, would it read better if point 4 were moved up, so that it comes between the new points 2 and 3? Well, maybe so. Let's try it. Hmmm, not bad but it's no big improvement either. Let's leave point 4 where it is. Finally, let's stand back from the outline one more time to see if it looks like the "right" skeleton for the piece of writing we want. If it doesn't, we'll probably have to go back to re-work the theme. Happily, it looks all right. So have we got our outline? Yes, indeed. We sure do.

Now what? We go on to the next step, which is writing out the first draft.

STEP THREE — Writing Out The First Draft:

When you've finished making your outline and begin to write out your first draft, the entire nature of the writing process changes. You go, so to speak, from design to construction. For most writers, this is a key turning point. Some writers find all the remaining steps — the construction steps, if you will — easier than the design steps. Other writers find these construction steps the hardest ones to take. There's very little you can do about this. It's entirely a matter of style, personality, skill, and preference. The trick to coping is simply to understand the shift that occurs at this point in the writing process; then you can either celebrate or, alas, make the best of it.

It's never easy to write a first draft, and anyone who says it is, is nuts. But the whole purpose of everything we have done up to now is to make this step a manageable one to take. In essence, you write a first draft by expanding, beefing up, and fleshing out your outline. As we said earlier, this is more of a construction job than it is a design job. So it's more a matter of effort than of inspiration. For those of you who would rather "think" than "work," writing a first draft will actually be a little boring and perhaps a bit tedious. And for those of you who despise "thinking" and prefer "working," writing a first draft will come as something of a relief, or even a bit of a lark.

The best advice we've ever heard for this particular step came, oddly enough, from a long-distance runner. Asked by a weekend jogger how on earth he had the energy and stamina to run twenty miles, the long-distance runner smiled and said: "Good heavens, I couldn't possibly get going if I thought about running twenty miles. I run one mile — but I do it twenty times."

You write a first draft by expanding, beefing up, and fleshing out one section of your outline at a time. You treat each section as though it were a separate entity, and you spend as much time as necessary with each section. Some will be easy to write; others will be hard. Some will come out so well, that when you settle down later on to polish your draft, these sections will need little if any work. Other sections will come out less well, and so will need more fixing up later on. You just do the best you can with a section, and when you're comfortable with that section — or in the case of hard sections, when you feel you've "had it" for the moment — you go on to the next section.

To begin, simply copy out the title and theme just as they appear in your outline:

The Switchover to Word Processors

Students at our college are in the midst of a switchover, from typewriters to word processors. The switchover is taking place because word processors are better, easier

*to use, and affordable. Students are making the trend
happen by buying their own machines, and the college
is helping. Moreover, the college is encouraging the trend.
We're heading for a time when all students will be using
word processors. On balance, the trend is a good one.*

Now, under your title and theme you expand, beef
up, and flesh out each section of your outline. Take
each section one at a time, and use each point -- that
is, each sentence or two that represents a section of
your outline — to launch the sections of your draft. If
your point is sound, you'll have no trouble carrying it
forward into a full paragraph or even into two or three
full paragraphs. After all, these paragraphs are merely
extensions, explanations, and elaborations of the outline
itself. Again, for convenience's sake continue to number
the sections:

*1. Students are switching over from typewriters to word
processors. Indeed, in the last few years students enrolled
at our college have begun to abandon their typewriters
for word processors. It's actually getting hard to find a
typewriter on campus now. Word processors may be
found in student dormitories, in classrooms, and in the
college library.*

What we've done here, as you can see, has been to
expand somewhat on the fact of the switchover trend.
By doing so, we have set the stage for the next section:

*2. The trend is taking place because word processors
are better than typewriters. For one thing, they are much
easier to use. Because the keyboards of word processors
are electronic, versus mechanical keyboards on typewriters, writing is much faster. Word processors make
it easy to change text, which saves time and energy.
Moreover, word processors have capabilities that typewriters don't have. You can tap into data banks with
word processors. And word processors are becoming more
affordable than they used to be.*

Notice how we've changed some of the wording from our outline. That's a perfectly correct — and quite common — thing to do. We made the changes so that our piece flowed more smoothly. Our objective was to expand, beef up, and flesh out what was in our outline. We did this by explaining how word processors are easier to use than typewriters, and what we meant when we said they have more capabilities than typewriters. Now we roll forward to the next section:

3. Students are making the trend happen by buying their own word processors. Some are bringing processors from home, but most are buying word processors here in town, at one of the two stores near campus which sell these machines. The college is helping students to make the switchover from typewriters to word processors in several ways. First, the college is providing a list of "acceptable" models, which means models that are compatible with the college's own computer system. Second, the college is making loans available to students who can't afford to buy processors on their own. And third, the college is offering instruction courses for students who own word processors but who are completely up a tree when it comes to using the things.

Professors are encouraging the trend toward word processors. They are doing this by allowing students to write their homework assignments on their word processors, then send the finished products to their professors electronically. The professors then grade the papers on their own word processors, and send back their comments and corrections also electronically. Some professors even allow students who own small, portable word processors to bring these machines into class, and to use them instead of pens and paper for taking notes.

We're rolling now, and as you can see we did quite a bit of beefing up and fleshing out. We told our reader where students are getting their word processors, and told our reader in some detail how the college is helping the switchover to happen. We even launched a second paragraph to tell how professors are encouraging the trend. After all, there's no reason to limit each section of our outline to just one paragraph; sometimes it will take two or three to do the job. In larger pieces of writing, such as books and theses, it sometimes takes pages or even chapters to accommodate each section of an outline. As a general rule, each section of your draft will be roughly equal in length to all the others. If the differences in length become really huge — say, by a factor or two or three — you're probably writing too much for the longer sections or, possibly, too little for the shorter ones. But this happens from time to time with first drafts; you can fix it later on, when you polish your product. This last section isn't too long compared with the earlier ones, so let's barrel forward:

4. As for where this trend is going, we're heading for a time when all students at the college will be using word processors. For one thing, students like word processors, and as more students become familiar with the machines more will buy them. In addition, the college itself is developing an extensive computer network, which means that students without word processors won't be able to take part in this network. That will make it difficult for them to compete with participating students. Moreover, prices are dropping steadily for word processors, which means that just about anyone who wants one will soon be able to afford one. It wouldn't be suprising if in a few years use of these machines will be required.

Not much to say about what we did here, except that we expanded our outline by explaining just why the use of word processors is likely to increase: students like them, the college itself is developing a computer network, prices are dropping steadily. The reader may be a bit startled to hear us say that the use of word processors may eventually be required; we really ought to tell him why we said it. Did someone we talked with on the faculty tip us off? Did we see a plan that included the required use of word processors? Or is it merely our own best judgment, based on everything we learned? We could stop right now, go back to the preceeding section, and fix this up. Or we could do it later on, when we polish the first draft. It really doesn't matter, so long as the job gets done. Let's decide to roll forward and not break our momentum:

5. It's clear that students who use word processors will be more efficient. They will be able to write faster, and have more of their energy and time available for reading, thinking, listening. And with word processors, students will be able to tap into all those data banks that are springing up, and that make so much information available so easily. There's really no end to the number of things that students can do with word processors. And new ones are being developed every day. So I believe the trend is a good one.

And so, we have a first draft. To be sure, it needs more work before we'd actually want to show it to anybody. It's a bit vague in places, slightly repetitious here and there, sorely in need of a few more details and examples, and in general too "thin" for comfort. But that's all right. Remember, in a first draft we are more concerned with architecture than with execution. As we read through it once again, we see that we have in fact succeeded in following the course of our outline by expanding, beefing up, and fleshing out the outline's points and sections. Indeed, despite the draft's drawbacks and shortcomings its theme, its direction, and its overall thrust are sharp and clear. Thus we have accomplished our key first-draft objective.

Most professional writers consider this to be a major milestone. Reaching it usually brings on an intense feeling of relief and even a wave or two of euphoria. Writers have been known to celebrate this milestone by taking the rest of the day off, by treating themselves to a special lunch or dinner, by buying themselves a present of some sort or — in extreme cases — by going out and getting dead drunk. We don't recommend this last alternative, but we've been known to try the others ourselves and they are not bad at all. So, at least for a little while, let yourself go. After all, with a first draft on paper, or on a computer diskette, the hard part is over.

And when you come back down to earth, you will be ready to go on to the third and final phase of the writing process, which is polishing your product. After running through the various skills and techniques required to turn your first draft into a finished product, we'll return to the trend report we've started and show how to carry it through to the end. You'll be pleasantly surprised by how easy it will seem.

Part Three

POLISHING
THE PRODUCT

In this third and final part of the writing process — polishing the product — your objective is to enhance, sharpen, and focus your draft to give it power and credibility. After all, a piece of writing is successful only when it does what the writer intends it to do — for instance when the piece of writing informs, or persuades, or convinces, or when it stimulates the reader to take whatever action the writer wants him or her to take. And to be successful a piece of writing must earn the reader's respect through its internal power and credibility. You can impart these qualities to your own first draft — whether it be a memo, a letter, an article, a term paper, a book, or any other writing product — by complying with the nine key guidelines of draft-polishing:

- Be accurate
- Be precise
- Be consistent
- Be brief
- Be fair
- Keep a steady depth
- Keep a steady tone
- Use an established layout
- Use good grammar

In working your way through these guidelines, you will have more flexibility than you've had up to now. In the first two parts of the writing process, you operated like an architect and then an engineer, first designing and then constructing your product. So you had no choice but to use a step-by-step approach, because you literally had to complete one step before going on to the next step. But now that all the floors are laid down and the walls up, so to speak, you can operate more in the manner of an interior decorator. A decorator can work his way swiftly through all the rooms of a house, first putting in the furniture, then going back through all the rooms and hanging all the curtains, then going back again to install the lamps and

once more for the appliances. Or, he can complete one
room before going on to the next one.

You have the same choice of approaches for polishing
your draft. In other words, there's no particular reason
to work your way systematically through each successive section, never moving forward to the next section
until you've applied all nine guidelines to whichever
section you're working on. You can if you want to, of
course. And many writers do. But if you prefer, you
can move swiftly from one section to the next, applying
just the first guideline to all the sections, then repeating
the process over and over, each time applying another
guideline, until you've applied all nine to the entire
draft. It makes no difference at all which way you do
it; it's entirely a matter of your own style and preference, as long as the job gets done.

Polishing the product, in addition to being the most
flexible part of the writing process, is also the most
variable part. It will either take the smallest chunk of
your total time, or the largest chunk. It depends on
three factors: the complexity of the piece you're writing,
the thoroughness of the draft you've turned out, and
the amount of time and energy you've got left when
you reach this part. Obviously, the more complex the
product you're writing, the more polishing you'll need
to do. For instance, a draft memo reminding people to
attend a meeting next Thursday isn't going to need
much polishing — or at least it shouldn't need much
polishing. But even a first-rate draft history of World
War II is likely to require months or even years of
effort to flesh out, refine, enhance. Moreover, if you
really skimmed your way through Parts One and Two,
you're likely to find that there's a fair amount of work
remaining to be done here in Part Three. On the other
hand, if you took your time and did a careful, thorough
job of organizing and drafting, much of what you would
have needed to do in this third part you already will
have done.

In all, polishing the product — rather like furnishing
a new house that you've designed and built yourself —
is often the most pleasant, satisfying part of the writing

process. For this is when you bring it all together, when you enhance your draft and turn it into something that's finished, complete, effective, and uniquely yours. To be precise, what you do is this: you go over your draft — once, twice, or several times as you prefer — making additions, deletions, and modifications to comply as best you can with these key guidelines:

BE ACCURATE:

Nothing discredits a piece of writing faster, or more thoroughly, than a mistake which the reader notices. As you polish your draft, you must assume that your reader will know at least something about your subject; that he or she will know one fact, one name, one title, one place, one incident, one — something. And if you the writer get this "something" wrong, there's a high risk your reader will conclude that the entire piece of writing is riddled with mistakes that he or she just hasn't caught; that its author is lazy or incompetent and that the piece of writing itself should be given the absolute minimum attention or perhaps even dismissed outright. Unfortunately, there is no way for you, the writer, to predict which one fact, name, title, place, incident, or whatever your reader will know. So you have no choice but to put in sufficient time and energy to get all of them right.

There are two kinds of accuracy: accuracy of fact and accuracy of description.

Accuracy of fact requires more effort than brilliance. It's largely a matter of looking it up, checking it out, getting it straight. For example, if for some reason you're writing about the Declaration of Independence that created the United States, you need only spend a moment with any almanac or history book to be certain that the Declaration came in 1776. If you write that it happened in any other year, you will lose all credibility no matter how thorough and perceptive your account may be of the Declaration itself or of the American Revolution. Or, if you're writing up a report of a meeting, you had better not describe John Jones as the company's treasurer if in fact he's the general counsel. You say you're not sure which title is correct? Call the man's office and ask, or get hold of the company's annual report and look it up yourself. And if you're writing about a woman who has successfully launched her own business, for heaven's sake don't say it's a pet-food company if in fact she's selling gourmet popcorn; don't describe her as tall if she's short, fat if she's thin, and the holder of an M.B.A. degree from the Harvard Business School if in fact she's a high-school dropout.

Check out facts yourself whenever possible. Get it wrong and the reader will hold you responsible, no matter where the fault really lies. If you write that the Declaration of Independence came in 1876, because that's what your sister's current boyfriend told you, you will have a mess on your hands. Not only won't your reader know who gave you wrong information, he or she won't care. You, and your piece of writing, will get the blame. Facts that can be checked out for certain must be checked out for certain. For example, the accuracy of every fact in this paragraph can be determined for certain by a writer:

The Happy Water Sailboat Company was founded in 1982 in Sag Harbor, New York. Sales during the first year of operation totaled $300,000, and doubled in 1984 to $600,000. The company now has sales offices in four locations throughout the region.

Of course, there are times when you do need to take somebody else's word for something. And at such times you protect yourself — that is, your own credibility and the credibility of whatever you're writing — by attributing facts that you cannot verify yourself directly to your source. For example:

According to Jenny Holmes, founder of the Happy Water Sailboat Company, the idea for the company emerged when friends in Sag Harbor told Ms. Holmes that they had tried to buy a boat that weekend and were disappointed to learn that there were no sailboat show-rooms anywhere in the town. After making her own investigation of the situation and her own projections of potential sales the company was formed, according to Ms. Holmes.

If Ms. Holmes turns out to have a rotten memory or, worse, to be a liar, that's too bad for her. But you the writer are protected — provided that you have accurately reported whatever she's said or claimed. When in doubt about whether or not a fact should be attributed to a source other than yourself, as a general rule go ahead and make the attribution. Your source need not always be a person:

This year teachers in our school district will earn $20,000, according to Thursday's edition of The Daily Globe.

The company's annual report claims that six new products were offered to the public during the previous year.

Ownership of the house changed hands four times during the past decade, according to records in the county clerk's office.

Accuracy of description is every bit as important as accuracy of fact—but a bit trickier to achieve. In essence, when you describe an incident, an event, even a person, you have to get the sense of it right. For instance, let's say that for some reason you are writing about the US Space Shuttle program. Every single report of Space Shuttle blast-offs that has ever been written or recorded (even the ill-fated *Challenger* mission) has described the crowds during count-down as tense, enthusiastic, fairly bursting with excitement. If your piece of writing uses words like "bored," "indifferent," and "complacent" to describe the count-down crowds — you're hopelessly off base. You haven't got the sense of it right at all. You're just plain wrong. Likewise if you should describe the Lincoln Memorial in Washington D.C. as "unimpressive," or President Ronald Reagan — universally recognized as one of the world's most cheerful and optimistic people — as a sad-eyed, morose pessimist. You can't say these things; they're just not true.

Accuracy of description has nothing whatever to do with personal judgment and opinion. You are entitled to any views you wish about the US Space Shuttle program, the Lincoln Memorial, or about President Reagan and the policies of his Administration, and of course you should express these views, if appropriate, in whatever you are writing. But when you are describing some thing, or some body, what you say must sound right to readers who have some idea of the truth, either from other pieces of writing, from other sources of information such as radio or television, or most importantly from their own personal experience.

It isn't always easy to "get the sense of it right." First, you must be careful to separate your personal judgment and opinion from the general perspective or recollection. For example, if you're writing up a report on a meeting of a university faculty that had been called to discuss whether students should be given the right to vote on their professors' requests for salary increases, you must set aside your own view of the issue long enough to report accurately how the meeting went. Did participants feel it was a good and useful meeting? Or did they consider it as a waste of time? Was the meeting harmonious or contentious? Was the mood angry? Cheerful? Businesslike? Sometimes you can "get the sense of it right" merely by staying alert during the proceedings. Other times you need to make an informal survey of participants.

Often it's just a matter of playing around with words and phrases until you find the ones that work best. Let's say you are trying to describe the taste of vanilla ice cream. Steer away from words like "delicious" and "awful," because these reflect personal opinion. Steer instead toward non-opinionated words like "smooth," "creamy," "cool," and "refreshing." In other words, you must scout around for words, or phrases, that describe accurately without also judging.

There is never any guarantee that a reader will accept your personal judgments and opinions. But you can be certain that if you fall short of total accuracy — both of fact and description — your readers will discredit whatever judgments and opinions you do express, however intelligent and valid they may be. So as you go about the business of polishing your draft keep in mind this rule: You are always entitled to your own judgments and opinions; you are never — never — entitled to your own facts. You have to use the real ones, and you have to get them right.

BE PRECISE:

Precision is a clear, direct reflection of how much effort a writer has devoted to his or her project. And because of this, readers tend to look kindly on pieces of writing that are consistently and visibly precise. By the same token, readers become uncomfortable and even downright snippy toward pieces of writing they judge to be imprecise. Fairly or not — and often without even realizing what they're doing — readers conclude that an imprecise writer has been lazy, and that the product itself isn't worth much attention. Simply put, then, the more precise your piece of writing is, the more willing your readers will be to accept or at least consider carefully your point of view. And you will be that much more likely to elicit from your readers the reaction or response that you want.

Precision is closely related to accuracy, but it is not quite the same thing. After all, you can be accurate but vague:

The first men to set foot on the moon landed there in the 1960s.

With a bit of effort you can be accurate and precise; with more effort you can be accurate and very precise:

The first men to set foot on the moon landed there in 1969.

The first men to set foot on the moon landed there on July 20, 1969.

Here's another set of examples, all accurate but each one more precise than the one before:

A senior official of the company voted against the chairman's proposal.

John Smith, a senior official of the company, voted against the chairman's proposal.

John Smith, executive vice president of the company, voted against the chairman's proposal.

John Smith, executive vice president of United Widget Corp., voted against the chairman's proposal.

John Smith, executive vice president of United Widget Corp., voted against the chairman's proposal to move corporate headquarters from Los Angeles to New York.

Just as with accuracy, there is precision of description as well as precision of fact. When you recount a concept, an idea, a program, a course of action — especially when it is someone else's — for the sake of your own credibility you have got to get the sense of it not only right, but precise. For example, this sentence is accurate but imprecise:

The mayor's program for reducing crime in the streets involves changes in the law itself and in the police department.

This is accurate and precise:

The mayor's program for reducing crime in the streets involves stiffer prison terms for convicted criminals and a 50 percent increase in the number of police officers assigned to neighborhood patrol duty.

Accurate:

The governor's anti-pollution program is a great success.

Accurate and precise:

The governor's anti-pollution program is a great success. Just two years after the program began, statistics show that our air and our water both are cleaner. According to the Committee For A Better Environment, at the present rate of improvement within three more years our air and water will be roughly twice as clean as they were before the program was launched.

As a general rule, readers want people that they read about to be identified with a high degree of precision — name, age, title if appropriate, home town:

John Harding, 45, chairman of Western Forge Company of Glendale, California, gave the keynote speech.

Police said the bank was robbed by Judy Caldwell, 34, an unemployed radio announcer from New York City.

You should identify a person only once, and you should always do it the first time that he or she is mentioned. After that, it's sufficient to use just the person's name. However, since people are curious about other people, it's always a good idea to offer your readers additional little tidbits of information whenever it's convenient and appropriate to do so. For instance, let's say that you're writing a newspaper article about a scholarship winner. The first time you mention this individual you would give just these key details:

Jimmy Johnson, 17, a senior at Western High School in Oak Grove, Louisiana, won a full scholarship to Harvard University.

But the next time you mention Jimmy Johnson, you could use the occasion to slip in an extra tidbit:

Johnson, who works on Saturday afternoons in his father's hardware store on Main Street, said Thursday that he plans to study biology.

If the extra tidbits you've slipped in seem all right, then let them remain in the text. But if you read through your text a second time and you decide you've put in too much information, go ahead and take some out. There are no hard and fast rules to cover this; your own judgment is really the best guide.

When describing concepts, ideas, proposed courses of action, and so forth, you must give enough information so that the reader can get a clear idea of what's involved. Moreover, by spelling out with precision a concept, an idea, or a proposed course of action, it becomes apparent to the reader that you — the writer — have devoted sufficient effort to know what you're talking about. And this, of course, helps to establish and maintain your own credibility:

The country has two political parties, the Yellows and the Blues. The Blues' program for reducing poverty rests primarily on use of the tax structure to transfer wealth from richer citizens to poorer citizens. More precisely, the Blues would raise taxes for families with incomes of $20,000 a year or more, then transfer this money to families with incomes of less than $20,000 a year through an assortment of social spending measures such as welfare payments and food stamps. The Blues haven't specified the amount of the middle-income and upper-income tax hikes that they would enact.

Or:

The Yellows' program for reducing poverty rests primarily on the idea of lowering taxes for everyone, and by doing so to trigger higher rates of economic growth. More precisely, the Yellows would cut taxes for all citizens a total of 30 percent over a three-year period, in hopes that people would both consume and invest the additional money in ways that would create new jobs and thus trigger a higher growth rate. This, in turn, would reduce the need for the social-spending measures, such as welfare payments and food stamps, that the Blues are advocating.

As you can see, once you get the hang of being precise there is almost no limit to the level of precision you can achieve. Obviously, you will need to apply some judgment. On the one hand, you never want to be too vague. On the other hand, you don't want to waste three pages describing a doorknob. In the majority of cases, you can achieve the right level of precision simply by following these two rules: First, be certain to give your reader enough detailed information to convince him or her that you, the writer, have done your homework and know what you're talking about. Second, put yourself in the reader's place and ask: What would I need to know about this person, this event, this idea, this program, this course of action, or whatever? What would I want to know? When the level of precision satisfies you, so too will it satisfy your readers.

BE CONSISTENT:

You can not expect to help somebody else make up his or her mind about something if you have not yet made up your own. So throughout your piece of writing, your personal judgments as well as your descriptions of people, events, and ideas must be internally consistent.

Judgments and descriptions that are mutually exclusive are not tolerable in any piece of writing. If in your first paragraph you describe an individual as "willful," you must be careful not to describe him or her three paragraphs later as "weak-minded." A house that is "beautiful" on the first page of your letter to Aunt Tilly cannot become a "hideous" or "ugly" house on page two. An event that is "exciting" at one point in your piece of writing cannot be "boring" in another. And a "revolutionary" idea at the beginning of your piece of writing cannot become a "long-standing, discredited" idea at the end.

Once again, the solution is to think before you write. Don't just leap on the first descriptive word that comes to mind. Give careful thought to your own perceptions of people, of events, of ideas. Reach your judgments slowly and carefully. But when you do reach them, stick to them all the way. If you read through a draft you've written and find conflicting judgments — that is, judgments that are not merely different, but mutually exclusive — you should realize what lies behind the problem. Namely, that you the writer have not yet made up your own mind or, worse, that you hold mutually exclusive views about something and simply haven't realized it. Ultimately, the solution is easy; you change one of the judgments or descriptions. But don't do it too quickly. First, stop to think about which judgment or description you really want; about which one truly reflects your own perception or point of view.

BE BRIEF:

Back in the nineteenth century — before television, before video tape recorders, before PacMan — families entertained themselves by reading aloud to one another. Naturally there was a huge appetite for reading material, and in England writers like Charles Dickens were hired by newspapers and magazines to spin out their stories in lengthy episodes that stretched across weeks and months. Since the objective was to help readers kill time, the longer the episodes the better. Dickens was actually paid according to the number of inches his work took up when published.

We live in a very different world. To be sure, reading the classics will always be among the greatest pleasures a civilized person can enjoy. But people don't have much time any more to read for pleasure. Most of the reading that most people do today is required reading. That is, people read mostly because they have to; because they need to absorb information. Indeed, this is the kind of reader we've been focusing on here in *HOW TO WRITE*.

When you're writing for someone who will read your product because he or she needs to read it, you want to take up as little of your reader's time and energy as necessary to do the job properly. In other words, you want to be brief.

The trick to being brief is to be utterly ruthless with yourself and with your draft. First, read through your draft and take out anything that is repetitious. Make your points well, but never make the same point twice. If you've fallen in love with the way you made a point the second time, stick with that formulation and eliminate the first one. Choose. Then read through your draft again to see if you've included the same fact twice. If you have, decide which place is best to include that fact and get rid of the other place.

Second, eliminate anything from your draft that is not directly relevant to your objective. This is often a painful thing to do, because "diversions" are often the most enjoyable and interesting parts of a draft. For example, if you're sending your boss a trip report on your meeting with an accounting firm in St. Louis, don't tell him about the movie star you sat next to on the airplane. At least, don't tell him in your report; tell him about it the next time you're both chatting at the water cooler. Keep your piece of writing on course at all times; save the detours for another day.

Curiously enough, it takes more effort to be brief than it does to ramble on. As the American humorist Ambrose Bierce once scribbled at the end of a letter to a friend, "Forgive me for writing such a long letter. I didn't have time to write a short one." And it isn't just the effort, it's the pain. Time and again you will find yourself removing good stuff not because it isn't good enough, but because it just doesn't belong there. This hurts, but you must force yourself to do it. Keep in mind that your reader will never know what you removed from your draft. All the reader knows is what ends up in the final product, and the less time and energy your reader needs to cope with that product the more likely you will be to achieve your objective.

BE FAIR:

Fairness in a person is admirable; in a piece of writing it is essential. That's because the absence of fairness stands out very clearly when you write; indeed it stands out far more clearly than when you speak. This is why the sort of flippant, off-hand comments you can get away with when you speak you simply cannot make when you write. For instance, you can get away with calling someone a horsethief in a conversation; do it in writing and you're in trouble — unless the individual literally has been convicted in a court of stealing a horse. Likewise, in a casual conversation you can brush off an idea you don't like as "dumb" or "stupid." In a piece of writing you would need to analyze the idea so that, in the end, your reader would come to understand why the idea is flawed or unworkable. In short, the standards for writing are much more strict than the standards for speaking. If the reader judges what you write to be unfair — it doesn't matter whether in fact this is a reasonable judgment; it matters only that the reader reaches this judgment — your ability is diminished to inform, to influence, to persuade, or to convince.

Being fair means including relevant facts even when they don't support the point you want to make. After all, you can support any point at all, no matter how vicious or idiotic, merely by including only those facts

that support the point you want to make and leaving
out everything else. For example:

*The United States is an evil country. Twice in this
century, it has fought in World Wars.*

Or:

*Vietnam is a good country. Its environmental laws
are strict, and there is very little industrial pollution.*

Even when the point you want to make is reasonable
and perfectly valid, it's a rare instance when all the
relevant facts support your point. Often you can gain
credibility by acknowledging evidence or conditions
that, so to speak, go in the wrong direction:

*Washington D.C. is a lovely city in which to live. The
buildings are beautiful, the residential neighborhoods
are pleasant, shopping is convenient, and the schools are
well run so the children are well protected from drug-
peddlers and other criminals. However, summers in
Washington are unbearable, as temperatures hover above
90 degrees with tropical-type humidity.*

Or:

*In sum, then, moving our headquarters from Man-
hattan out to suburban Westchester County will have
several advantages. Our office rental costs would be
lower, our employees, most of whom live in Westchester
now, would have shorter commutes to work, we would
be closer to our markets in New England, and local tax
rates would be lower than in Manhattan. On the other
hand, by leaving New York City we would distance
ourselves from our three prime competitors, all of whom
are in Manhattan. Thus it would be harder for us to
know what they are up to. Moreover, since many of our
officers will need to visit New York customers regularly,
they would need to spend quite a bit of time traveling*

back and forth from Manhattan to our headquarters in Westchester County.

Never be afraid to include a relevant fact just because it doesn't support your argument. As long as your argument is sound, and as long as you include all the necessary facts to show your reader that it's sound, there's no danger that your reader will suddenly turn on you. Indeed, the danger is that your reader will discover the contrary fact by him- or herself — and will wonder how come it never occurred to you. Remember, you can never be certain that your piece of writing is the only piece your reader will read before making up his or her mind. In essence, when you write you want not simply to tell your reader *what* to think about a subject, but rather you want to show your reader *how* to think about a subject. You want to show all the facts that you took into account — and which, therefore, your reader should take into account — in reaching your own conclusions.

Being fair also means reporting the existence of opinions other than your own. This is an especially vital thing to do when your judgment or opinion is unique or at least uncommon:

"WAR AND PEACE" is the most boring novel I have ever read. It's much too long, the author goes on for page after page describing things of absolutely no interest, and of the dozens of characters in the book there is not one that I find attractive or sympathetic. To be sure, "WAR AND PEACE" is widely acclaimed as one of the greatest novels of all time, largely because of its historic sweep and what many critics consider the overwhelming power of its prose. But in my view the novel's drawbacks exceed its strengths.

Or:

I have decided to end our system of assigned parking places. I realize that most of you like the present system, on the grounds that each of you knows where his parking

space will be no matter what time you arrive for work,
and that you therefore oppose this change. But after due
consideration I remain convinced that a first-come, first-
served parking space system will be more fair and more
efficient since it will reward those who arrive early and
penalize those who show up late.

Your readers will find a unique or unpopular opinion
or decision much easier to take if you acknowledge its
uniqueness or unpopularity. Doing so suggests that you
have considered the alternatives, and have decided to
stick with your opinion or go ahead with your decision
anyway. This implies conviction, which in turn earns
credibility.

Finally, being fair means taking circumstances into
account. Remember, when you write you are the eyes
and ears of your reader. He or she is relying on you,
through your piece of writing, to present a balanced
picture or point of view:

Bill Harper's presentation to our Civic Improvement
Society was not as sharply focused as we had hoped.
Moreover, during the question-and-answer session after
his presentation Bill was curt and even rude to some
members of the audience. In sum, we were extremely
disappointed and more than a little angry. To be sure,
we later learned that one of Bill's children had entered
the hospital just that morning; this may well have ac-
counted for Bill's performance.

Of course, being fair does not invariably mean you
must excuse everything or everyone you criticize. Take
out the final sentence of the above paragraph, facts
permitting, and with this substitution the paragraph
would end with a very different tone:

This is not the first time Bill has performed in an
unsatisfactory manner. I've checked with several people
who attended his last three presentations, and they all
report that Bill seemed unprepared, and that he was
curt and rude to members of his audiences. Moreover,

there are no special circumstances that I can find to explain this away. Clearly, then, Bill's latest performance is part of an inexcusable trend.

Again, being fair does not mean being kind, or agreeing with every imaginable opinion or point of view. It simply means taking circumstances into account and reporting these circumstances to your reader so that he or she can see that your judgments are based on a genuine understanding of the situation or the issue.

Always keep in mind how important it is to earn and keep your reader's respect — and how easy it is to lose this respect by not being fair. When you find yourself reluctant to include a relevant fact you know that fairness requires be included — and this happens to every writer now and then — it usually means your argument is weak or otherwise badly flawed and that deep down you know it. The solution is not to fight the problem or to ignore it, but rather to face the problem and deal with it.

KEEP A STEADY DEPTH:

Imagine walking into an electronics store in search of some equipment for your home. As you browse through the displays, you discover that the store offers six models of videotape recorders, twelve models of radios, nine models of record players — and one model television set. The experience is annoying, to say the least. After all, we expect a store to maintain a certain balance in its stock of merchandise. So too with pieces of writing, and in writing this balance of merchandise that we expect is called depth.

All pieces of writing have a certain depth. One difference between good and bad pieces of writing is that in good pieces, the depth holds steady all the way through. A bad piece of writing is one in which the depth fluctuates. For example, a book on US history during the twentieth century that has two hundred pages about World War I and two hundred pages about the Great Depression, should not have just five pages about World War II.

Choosing the proper depth for your piece of writing is among the key decisions you need to make. There is no rule for doing this, except the obvious: you give your reader as much detail as necessary to accomplish your ends. Instinct and common sense usually do the trick. The problem usually comes somewhere in the middle of a draft, when for some reason the writer changes depth either by going deeper — giving too much detail about a particular incident, point, person, idea — or by rising up to a more shallow depth — which is to say giving too few details about a particular incident, point, person, idea. It isn't that one depth is necessarily better than the other; it's the very fact of the change that unsettles the reader. For example:

Present at the meeting were John Smith, a teacher from Akron, Ohio; Hazel Hawkins, a chemical engineer from Tallahassee, Florida, Gerald Williams, an electrician from Rochester, New York; and Howard Snelling, 45, a lawyer from San Francisco who is a graduate of Yale University, served for three years as a lieutenant in the US Marine Corps, spent twelve years with the Global Construction Company, and who in 1982 placed third in the Boston Marathon.

It is just as unsettling to a reader when the depth of a piece of writing changes in the opposite direction. That is, when it suddenly rises up to a more shallow level:

In sum, there are three houses in this neighborhood suitable for your family and within the price range you have selected. The first is a three-bedroom brick townhouse on Oak Street, built in 1965 with gas heating and central air conditioning. Its kitchen has just been remodeled, all the rooms have wall-to-wall carpeting, and local taxes are $1,500 a year. The second house is a four-bedroom colonial on Elm Street, built of wood and aluminum siding in 1963. It uses oil heat, has four room

*air conditioners, a large family room downstairs, and
an apartment with a separate entrance that is currently
rented for $200 per month. Local taxes last year totaled
$1,200. The third possibility is a ranch house with a
backyard.*

In lengthy pieces of writing, you hold a steady depth
all the way through by giving equal weight to facts,
events, people, and ideas that are equally important to
whatever you are writing. For instance, in a book about
World War II you would certainly need to talk about
World War I and the Great Depression, since each was
among the causes of the latter conflict. But you would
not need to discuss World War I and the Great Depression in the same detail as you would need to discuss
the book's main subject, World War II. However, you
would discuss World War I and the Great Depression
in equal detail, if you are contending that each con-
tributed equally to World War II. And within your
discussion of World War II, you would give equal
treatment to battles that you judge to be equally sig-
nificant.

Different writers have different approaches to this
need for setting and holding a steady depth. Some turn
out first drafts that, in general, have far too much depth.
Others turn out first drafts that, in general, are too
shallow. When polishing their drafts, those writers in
the first category find themselves removing details here
and there, while those in the second category find themselves adding details here and there. Neither approach
is necessarily better than the other; as so often is the
case, it's merely a question of personal style. All that
matters is that at some point during the writing process
you select an appropriate depth and then hold it steady
all the way through.

KEEP A STEADY TONE:

So similar is the tone issue to the depth issue that
you could re-read the preceding section, substituting

tone for depth, and have it just about right. Very briefly, then, every piece of writing has a tone: serious, flippant, formal, informal, aggressive, friendly, forceful, gentle, nasty, cheerful, and so forth. You can choose whatever tone you want — whichever one you find most appropriate, most comfortable, and which you believe will achieve the goals of your particular piece of writing. But once you make this choice, you must stick with it all the way through. You can't change your mind — that is, your tone — in the middle. A change of tone is as easy to recognize as a change of depth:

Dear Representative Holden,

I am writing to protest your vote last Thursday, in which you opposed the President's defense budget. I believe a strong defense is absolutely vital to protect our national security, and it is because the President shares this view that I have supported him throughout his Administration. Your vote against higher defense spending will encourage our nation's enemies to believe that we no longer have the will to defend our society. Thus I urge you to reconsider your position on this important issue. Should you hold to your present position, I cannot guarantee my support in your next election. Besides, your speech on this subject was a real stinker; I don't know how you can say such garbage. Maybe you're crazy.

Or:

Dear Joe,

Are you crazy? Why in heaven's name did you vote against the President's defense bill last Thursday? You know as well as I do that a strong defense is absolutely vital to our national security. Besides, votes like yours only encourage the Russians to think they can walk all over us. And Joe, that speech of yours was a real stinker. Do us both a favor and give this issue some more thought. However, in the event that you choose to persist with your present line of voting, I must warn you that neither

*I nor my family will support you in your next election
campaign. I trust, therefore, that you will take this matter under careful advisement.*

Choosing the right tone in the first place is fairly
easy. It requires merely that you have some sense of
occasion. That is, use precisely the tone you would use
if you were talking to the individual who will be your
reader. The better you know the intended reader —
and the better the reader knows you — the less formal
you likely will be. Of course, in many pieces of writing
you will choose a tone that is really a combination of
tones: friendly but furious, formal but cheerful, dignified but indignant, and so forth. Use whatever tone
makes you comfortable; your instinct will nearly always
be good. Just read through your first draft to see what
tone you have in fact selected. If it strikes you as the
wrong tone, change it immediately. If you're comfortable with the tone you've chosen, as you polish your
draft just make certain to hold that tone all the way
through.

USE AN ESTABLISHED LAYOUT:

In writing, as in everything else, presentation matters
hugely. Present something well, and its merits become
more visible than its flaws. Present something badly,
and its weaknesses show up more clearly than its
strengths. In writing, the technical word for presentation is "layout." It simply means the physical design
and appearance of your product.

There are no ironclad laws that govern the layouts
for pieces of writing in all the different categories —
sales brochures, technical papers, book reviews, letters
of inquiry or complaint, newspaper and magazine articles, notices to employees, reports of meetings, high-
school themes, college essays, how-to books, and so
forth. Nor are there any hard-and-fast rules that dictate
the size or color of paper to use, the typeface style, the
correct width of lines or number of lines per page, or,

for instance, whether to put the date on a letter you're writing at the top of the page or at the bottom, against the left margin or against the right.

But there's no need to design from scratch your own layout for whatever you're writing. For one thing, the choice of layout very often does not belong to the writer. After all, when you submit something for publication in a newspaper or magazine, it's not you the writer but the editor who needs to choose a layout. All you the writer need do is send in your finished, polished piece of writing in a clear, legible form. You really don't have any layout decisions to make at all. But even when you the writer are submitting the finished product without an editor or middleman of some sort to handle the layout — for example when you're writing a letter, or a memo, or an essay of some sort for school — there's no need to design a layout from scratch. For no matter what category your own piece of writing falls into, it's a category that has been around for a long time, and one for which through trial and error effective layouts have long since been established.

This is one time when it makes good sense to take the easy way out. Literally get your hands on several pieces of writing in your category that have already been done by other people. For instance, if you're writing a letter requesting a job interview, get your hands on some job-interview letters that other people have written. Or if you're writing up a report on this week's meeting of the annual-picnic committee, ask around to see if the report on last week's meeting is available, or if the files from last year's venture are still around. You should not be the slightest bit embarrassed to do this. First, it makes sense and doing the sensible thing is never wrong. Second, you can bet your life that the people who wrote the examples you are collecting themselves did precisely the same thing. Don't you think we went around libraries and bookstores, browsing through and buying up all sorts of "how-to" books, before deciding on the layout for this one? Of course we did; we would have been foolish not to have done so.

Happily, for a growing number of writing categories, very specific "how-to" books and pamphlets are now available in most libraries and bookstores. You can find books and pamphlets devoted exclusively to the subjects of how to write resumes, business letters, technical papers, doctoral theses, and all sorts of writing categories. While the quality of these books and pamphlets varies, most provide excellent illustrative examples of the most effective, established layouts for their respective categories. These books and pamphlets will be especially useful if you aren't able to put your hands on "real" examples.

Again, there are no ironclad laws, no hard-and-fast rules. So in theory, you can design any layout you want. But the established layouts work; that's why they have become established. So go ahead and collect some examples, browse through them, and when you find the one that seems most comfortable to you and most effective for the piece you're writing and for the reader you have in mind — simply duplicate the layout. Of course, you may want to make some minor changes in the layout you've selected to suit your own unique purpose and audience. Go right ahead. When you've finished, if your own piece of writing looks well presented to you, so too will it look well presented to your reader.

USE GOOD GRAMMAR:

You were probably beginning to think that we were going to make it all the way to the end of this book without once mentioning the most dreaded word in all the world of writing: grammar. Well, sorry but here we go. Grammar — which means the proper use of words and punctuation to construct sentences — is important. In any language, the established rules of grammar make it easier to communicate simply because these rules are established, which is to say they are widely accepted and understood. Obviously, the better your own command of these rules — your command of grammar — the easier it is for others to grasp your point. Can you communicate without total or near-total command of your language's grammar? Of course you can, and people do. But it's harder — that is, it requires more effort by those you are communicating with — and so your ability to communicate effectively is diminished. Put another way, the weaker your grammar the greater the burden on your reader to grasp your point. And the harder it is for someone to grasp your point, the less likely you are to succeed — that is, to communicate effectively — no matter how good your point may be.

There is no language in the world whose rules of grammar are too hard for the overwhelming majority of people to learn. After all, everybody learns to talk well enough to communicate. And the rules of grammar that apply to speech are precisely the same as those for writing. The only difference, as we've said before, is that for obvious reasons grammatical errors show up more starkly in writing than in speaking. So the need to be correct when you write is greater than the need to be correct when you speak. This explains why most schools in most countries, when they teach writing, put so much emphasis on teaching the rules of grammar. In theory, then, by the time you finish school you should know the rules of grammar in your language. If you don't, in all likelihood it's the school's fault. After all, you already knew how to talk when you arrived at school. All the school needed to do was to fine-tune and perhaps reinforce what you already knew.

Nevertheless, if you don't have a firm grip on the rules of grammar now — when you need to write something — you have a problem that must be solved quickly. It would take a book ten times the size of this one to sketch out all the rules of grammar, to give examples, and to explain all the tricky details well enough to give you a firm grip on the subject. Happily, dozens of such book are easily available, and you should get your hands on one immediately if poor grammar is your special problem.

Whether or not you use a grammar book, checking

your piece of writing for grammatical errors should always be the very last thing you do before sending your finished product on its way to your intended reader or readers. The chances are that you, like most people, use better grammar when you talk than when you write. One trick to catching grammatical errors in your writing product is simply to read the piece out loud, as though you were talking it out to your reader. If something suddenly sounds off-key, it's a good bet you've made a grammatical error. If you can see how to fix it, go ahead. If you can't see how to fix it, consult whatever grammar book you're using or, in a pinch, ask a friend or colleague for help. Again, don't be embarrassed to ask for help; you'll be more embarrassed if your product goes forward with a grammatical mistake in it.

As you can see from all these guidelines, polishing your product requires a combination of judgment and applied technique. Your objective is to smooth out the rough edges, fill in the cracks, bolster weak sections and generally balance the whole product so that your reader will find it easy to absorb your information and, ultimately, your point. How you do all this is your business, dependent wholly on your style and taste. You can apply one guideline to all the sections of your draft, then start from the beginning again with the second guideline then again with the third, fourth, and so on. Or you can apply all the guidelines to the first section, going on to the second section only when the first is fully polished, then so on through all the subsequent sections of your draft. Keep in mind, of course, that in most cases you won't need to modify each section to accommodate all the guidelines. In all likelihood, you will have only one or two flaws in each draft section. That is, Section One might need more precision and better grammar, while Section Two will need a touch of accuracy and Section Four will have a depth or tone problem.

To show you just what all this really looks like, let's

go back to our draft of *The Switchover to Word Processors*, which we developed in Part Two. First, we'll repeat the draft of each section exactly as it appears in Part Two. Then we'll write out a polished version of this same section. We will follow this, in turn, with an explanation of why we made each change in the first draft — of which particular guideline led us to make each particular change in the text. We'll repeat this one-two-three pattern for each section, so you can really see how to polish a draft and what a finished product looks like. Mostly in the interest of saving space — but also because it suits our own style and taste — we'll use the second approach to draft-polishing. That is, we'll apply all the guidelines to each section before going on to the next one:

THEME

Draft Version:

Students at our college are in the midst of a switchover, from typewriters to word processors. The switchover is taking place because word processors are better, easier to use, and affordable. Students are making the trend happen by buying their own machines, and the college is helping. Moreover, the college is encouraging the trend. We're heading for a time when all students will be using word processors. On balance, the trend is a good one.

Polished Version:

Students at our college are in the midst of a switchover, from typewriters to word processors. The switchover is taking place because word processors are better, easier to use, and affordable. Students are making the trend happen by buying their own machines, and the college is helping. Moreover, the college is encouraging the trend.

We're heading for a time when all students will be using word processors. On balance, the trend is a good one.

Reasons for Changes:

As you can see, we didn't make any changes. This isn't suprising, because we fussed a great deal with our theme when we drafted it. It had to be just right, so we honed it several times even before we made our outline. As a general rule, you hone a theme so carefully when you draft it that little if any polishing is ever needed. It's the succeeding sections that need most of the polishing for accuracy, precision, consistency, fairness, and so forth. So as you read through your theme when you settle down to polish your draft, just make certain that the grammar is correct. Save your polishing efforts for what follows.

SECTION ONE

Draft Version:

Students are switching over from typewriters to word processors. Indeed, in the last few years students enrolled at our college have begun to abandon their typewriters for word processors. It's actually getting hard to find a typewriter on campus now. Word processors may be found in student dormitories, in classrooms, and in the college library.

Polished Version:

Students are switching over from typewriters to word processors. In the last few years about 60 percent of our students have made this switchover, according to the chairman of our computer-sciences department. It's actually getting hard to find a typewriter on campus now. Word processors may be found in nearly all our student dormitories, in most of our classrooms, and in the college library — where there are 12 word processors including six IBMs, four Apples, and two Commodores, all located in the study hall on the East side of the second floor.

Reasons for Changes:

1. For the sake of being concise, we took out the second sentence of the draft version; it was just a repeat of the first sentence using different words.

2. To build in more precision, we wrote out the percentage of students who now have word processors, and for accuracy's sake we attributed this statistic to our source, the chairman of the computer-sciences faculty.

3. Again to be more precise, we changed the last sentence to show just where word processors may be found on campus.

SECTION TWO

Draft Version:

The trend is taking place because word processors are better than typewriters. For one thing, they are much easier to use. Because the keyboards are electronic, versus mechanical keyboards on typewriters, writing is much faster. Word processors make it easy to change text, which saves time and energy. Moreover, word processors have capabilities that typewriters don't have. You can tap into data banks with word processors. And word processors are becoming more affordable than they used to be.

Polished Version:

The trend is taking place because students like word processors better than typewriters. For one thing, they are much easier to use. Because the keyboards are electronic, versus mechanical keyboards on typewriters, writing is much faster. For example, it takes about three minutes to type a page, versus just two minutes when *using a word processor. Word processors make it easy to change text — to delete words or sentences, to insert them, to shift the order of them — which saves time and energy. Moreover, word processors have capabilities that typewriters don't have. You can tap into data banks with word processors. And word processors are becoming more affordable than they used to be. A machine that would have cost between $4,000 and $5,000 just three years ago costs just $1,500 to $2,000 today, according to James Blimp, who owns a local computer store.*

Reasons for Changes:

1. We inserted the phrase "students like" in the first sentence, referring to word processors, because it's the more accurate way to explain why the trend is taking place.

2. We added a sentence to show just how much faster a word processor is than a typewriter. That's a way to be more precise.

3. In the very next sentence — also for precision's sake — we added some details that show how a word processor makes writing easier.

4. And we added one final sentence — yet again for precision's sake — to show just how affordable word processors have become.

SECTION THREE

Draft Version:

Students are making the trend happen by buying their own word processors. Some are bringing processors from home, but most are buying word processors here in town, at one of the two stores near campus which sell these machines. The college is helping students to make the switchover from typewriters to word processors in several ways. First, the college is providing a list of "acceptable" models, which means models that are compatible with the college's own computer system. Second, the college is making loans available to students who can't afford to buy processors on their own. And third, the college is offering instruction courses for students who own word processors but who are completely up a tree when it comes to using the things.

Professors are encouraging the trend toward word processors. They are doing this by allowing students to write their homework assignments on their word processors, then send the finished products to their professors electronically. The professors then grade the papers on their own word processors, and send back their comments and corrections also electronically. Some professors even allow students who own small, portable word processors to bring these machines into class, and to use them instead of pens and paper for taking notes.

Polished Version:

Students are making the trend happen by buying their own word processors. Some are bringing processors from home, but most are buying word processors here in town, at one of the two stores near campus which sell these machines. The college is helping students to make the switchover from typewriters to word processors in several ways. First, the college is providing a list of "acceptable" models, which means models that are compatible with the college's own computer system. Second, the college is making loans available to students who can't afford to buy processors on their own. And third, the college is offering instruction courses for students who own word processors but need some help in learning how to use the things.

Professors are encouraging the trend toward word processors. They are doing this by allowing students to write their homework assignments on their word processors, then send the finished products to their professors electronically. The professors then grade the papers on their own word processors, and send back their comments and corrections also electronically. Some professors even allow students who own small, portable word processors to bring these machines into class, and to use them instead of pens and paper for taking notes.

Reasons for Changes:

1. We only made one change in this entire section, but it was an important one. In the last sentence of the first paragraph, we took out the phrase *"students who own word processors but who are completely up a tree when it comes to using the things,"* and substituted the phrase *"students who own word processors but need some help in learning how to use the things."* The draft sentence projects a very different tone from the rest of the trend report; it's a tone much more suitable to two students chatting over lunch than to a faculty member writing in the alumni bulletin. The polished phrase is more appropriate; it reflects the informal but dignified tone we chose at the start.

SECTION FOUR

Draft Version:

As for where this trend is going, we're heading for a time when all students at the college will be using word processors. For one thing, students like word processors, and as more students become familiar with the machines more will buy them. In addition, the college itself is developing an extensive computer network, which means that students without word processors won't be able to take part in this network. That will make it difficult for them to compete with participating students. Moreover, prices are dropping steadily for word processors, which means that just about anyone who wants one will soon be able to afford one. It wouldn't be surprising if in a few years use of these machines will be required.

Polished Version:

We're heading for a time when all students at the college will be using word processors. Students like word processors, and as more of them become familiar with the machines more will buy them. In addition, the college is developing an extensive computer network, which means that students without word processors won't be able to take part in this network. That will make it difficult for them to compete academically with participating students. Moreover, prices are continuing to drop steadily for word processors, which means that just about anyone who wants one will soon be able to afford one. It wouldn't be surprising if in a few years the use of these machines will be required.

Reasons for Changes:

1. For brevity's sake, we got rid of the opening phrase "*As for where this trend is going . . .* " It's just not necessary. For this same reason, we cut out the phrase "*For one thing*" from the second sentence.

2. Later on, in the sentence about the problems of students without word processors, we inserted one word in the phrase "*that will make it difficult for them to compete with participating students*" so that it reads "*difficult for them to compete academically with participating students.*" By adding the word "academically" we made the sentence more accurate.

SECTION FIVE

Draft Version:

It's clear that students who use word processors will be more efficient. They will be able to write faster, and have more of their energy and time available for reading, thinking, listening. And with word processors, students will be able to tap into all those data banks that are springing up, and that make so much information avail-

able so easily. There's really no end to the number of things that students can do with word processors. And new uses are being developed every day. So I believe the trend is a good one.

Polished Version:

It's clear that students who use word processors will be more efficient. They will be able to write faster, and have more of their energy and time available for reading, thinking, listening. And with word processors, students will be able to tap into all those data banks that are springing up, and that make so much information available so easily. To be sure, these machines are no more than a tool. They are not a substitute for thinking, reading, working. This means there is always a danger that students with word processors will become lazy. We'll need to pay attention, to make sure this doesn't happen. But the benefits of word processors far outweigh the potential drawbacks. So on balance I believe the trend is a good one

Reasons for Changes:

1. We made some big changes in this section. In the interest of being brief, we took out two entire sentences: *"There's really no end to the number of things that students can do with word processors. And new ones are being developed every day."* These sentences added nothing to our draft except a few lines of type; they made no real point, and when we wrote them we were just blathering on.

2. We included four new sentences: *"To be sure, these machines are no more than a tool. They are not a substitute for thinking, reading, working. This means there is always a danger that students with word processors will become lazy. We'll need to pay attention, to make sure this doesn't happen."* We included these sentences to be fair — to present the other side of the argument. We wanted our reader to know that we had thought seriously about the theme of our trend report — the

switchover to computers — and that we understood it thoroughly. And these four sentences required us to add the fifth and then to slightly modify the final sentence: *"But the benefits of word processors far outweigh the potential drawbacks. So on balance . . . "*

As you see, polishing our draft was quite a project. Once we got past our theme, we made at least one change in each section. Interestingly, nearly half our changes were made to accommodate the same guideline: be precise. That's because our own style is to move briskly through a draft, turning one out that is rather on the thin side. So we always need to flesh out and beef up our drafts, and we do that by making our general statements or assertions more precise. Other writers tend to "over-write." That is, they turn out drafts that are much too long and too detailed. Their primary polishing chore is to thin out their drafts by cutting them down to size. As we've said, it doesn't matter how you prefer to work, as long as the polished product comes out properly.

Like most writers, we're never quite satisfied with our work. We always want to make one more change, and as long as time permits there's no reason not to go over a polished draft one more time. We've just done that — and we've found something we should have seen earlier. Look at the last sentence of Section One, as it appears after polishing: *"Word processors may be found in nearly all our student dormitories, in most of our classrooms, and in the college library — where there are 12 word processors, including six IBM's, four Apples, and two Commodores, all located in the study hall on the East side of the second floor."* We're embarrassed to admit it, but at the end of this sentence we changed our depth rather drastically. We gave much too much information about the word processors in the library, and on second glance — actually, on third glance — we realized what we had done. The solution is simple: we could end the sentence after the word *"library"* or after the phrase *"where there are 12 word processors."* Either choice would work, and we chose the latter.

Now that we've gone through all the sections of our draft, and polished them as best we can, the next step is to make certain that our product fits into an established layout. As it happens, this is no problem at all for the particular piece we've been writing. Remember, we said this was going to be an article for a college alumni bulletin, which means the layout will be established by that bulletin's editor. So all we need do now is make sure that the final product is written out or typed clearly and legibly.

There is just one more step to take before we're done. If at all possible, when we finish polishing our draft we should go away from it. We should get a cup of coffee or a glass of milk, take a walk around the block, go for a jog or a bike ride, call on our friends or play with our children — anything that will help us to relax and clear our minds. We have just been through an arduous process, one that is difficult and draining even for the most experienced, professional writers. Then, when we're feeling up to it, we'll take one final look at our product. If we can see something that needs fixing — a misspelled word here, a grammatical error there, a poorly written phrase somewhere else, a missing example or even one example too many — we'll go ahead and make the necessary change.

But that's it. We will have reached the point of diminishing returns, and any changes we make after that are just as likely to weaken our piece of writing as to strengthen it. We must accept the fact that with more time, and more experience, we could have done better. But we've done the best we can, and we've done it by working in an orderly, sensible fashion. Now it's time to send our piece of writing forward. We've worked our way through the process outlined here in *HOW TO WRITE*, so our reader should have no difficulty whatever grasping what we mean to say. And enabling our reader to grasp our meaning is what matters most. So there's nothing left to do but put down our pen or pencil, or turn off our word processor. We've succeeded.

READY, SET, GO

As we said at the outset, *HOW TO WRITE* is a handbook. So keep it handy, and use it to guide yourself through whatever it is you need to write. Above all, remember that writing is a process. So don't be surprised — or disappointed — if some or even all of the steps we've outlined in Parts One, Two, and Three seem awkward or difficult your first time out. All processes take a bit of time and experience to master. After you've worked your way through one or two actual writing projects, you will find these steps less awkward and much easier to take. Indeed, as you become familiar with your own strengths and weaknesses, and with your own work habits, you'll find yourself moving swiftly through some steps and, as you continue to pick up speed and to gain experience, even combining steps along the way.

Alas, we can't be there to answer questions while you work. But to help you get started, we've pulled together this series of questions and answers:

When I write, I just can't sit still long enough to go through all the steps you've outlined. I lose my concentration too quickly. What do I do about this?

You've hit upon a key point about the writing process: it's exhausting, both physically and mentally. You should expect to run out of gas from time to time as you work your way through the various steps. Sometimes you'll be able to work your way through several steps before your concentration falters. Other times one single step will be so difficult, so downright tiring, that completing this one step will be as much as you can do.

There is absolutely no way to prevent an attack of "writer's fatigue". It's like the flu; when it hits, it hits. With experience you'll learn to recognize the signs of a coming attack: your concentration begins to flag, you lose your mental focus and for a moment can't remember what point you were trying to make, you find yourself writing something that is so silly, so utterly useless that you can't believe you just wrote it. As we say, there's no way to prevent an attack of "writer's fatigue." However, there is a cure: you do absolutely nothing except to relax, accept the fact that you've got to stop for a while, and you go do something else — anything else — until you're ready and able to start work again. For short pieces of writing, a five-minute or ten-minute break usually does the trick. For longer pieces of writing, you'll need an hour or two. Indeed, it's quite common for professional writers to knock off work for the day when "writer's fatigue" strikes, even if it's late morning or early afternoon (provided some good work has been done). For really lengthy, complex pieces of writing — books, theses, major analytic or technical essays — it can take days or even weeks for "writer's fatigue" to pass.

Our advice is this: When you feel an attack of "writer's fatigue" coming on, don't fight it. Accept the attack for what it is, and take a break. In the long run you'll actually save time, since if you try to keep working through an attack you'll write such garbage, and even goof up whatever good material you'd already written, that it would take twice as long to untangle the mess as it would to make up for lost time. Second, anticipate these attacks; they happen to everyone now and then. So as you set about your project and plan your work schedule, leave some room for "downtime." Finally, when the attack comes do whatever works for you to put your writing project out of mind — read a spy novel, paint the garage, ride your bike, listen to music, go to a movie, whatever. Just remember that taking a break to clear the cobwebs out of your brain and to re-charge your batteries is part and parcel of the writing process. So don't feel guilty about enjoying yourself when you think you should be "working."

I understand everything you've said. But somehow I still have trouble getting started. What exactly is the absolute, first thing to do when I launch a writing project?

The absolute, first thing to do when you launch a writing project is to resist the impulse to start writing. You need to relax, to settle down, and above all YOU NEED TO THINK. Don't worry about wasting time; it's never a waste of time to get your thoughts in order. Who has asked you to write something? Who will read it? What purpose is the piece of writing intended to serve? To persuade? To inform? To trigger action of one sort or another? Ask yourself all these questions, and don't settle for the first answers that pop into your head. And when you feel you've got it right, then — and only then — should you move on to the first real step in the writing process: deciding what it is you're going to write by choosing the correct category of writing product.

Your notion of using imaginary conversations at key points in the writing process; I'm not quite clear on it. Why should we do it? What's the big advantage?

The purpose of any piece of writing, in any category, is to communicate with someone. Most people find it easier to communicate in person than on paper; to talk rather than to write. Moreover, a piece of writing succeeds only when it's pitched precisely to its intended audience — to the actual person or persons for whom it's being written. By holding an imaginary conversation with your intended reader, you push toward both objectives. First, by talking out your piece of writing you leap over the period of stiffness or even paralysis that often accompanies an effort to start writing. Second, you begin to focus sharply on your intended reader or readers; to really see him, her, or them clearly and to understand what it is they need from whatever you plan to write.

My problem is length. How long is a piece of writing supposed to be?

Everybody worries about length, and everybody is wrong. Length is a non-problem. Your piece of writing — whether a thank-you note to Aunt Sally or a history of the automobile industry — should be just as long, and no longer, than it takes to say whatever you need and want to say. That, and only that, is the "correct" length for any piece of writing. Quite literally, there are no rules about length. Look in any library or bookstore, and you'll find books ranging from thirty-five pages long to several volumes. We've seen business memos that were just a single paragraph, and memos that approached book length; what matters is the substance and the layout, and nothing else.

But what about the length of individual sections of a piece of writing?

Same thing. There are no rules as such, provided you keep a steady depth all the way through. Just make certain that when you get to working out your layout, whatever you come up with is comfortable for your reader's eyes. You don't want the poor devil to go blind staring at a page of solid text, which is why on extended pieces of writing you ought to have at least two paragraphs on each page.

What's the absolute minimum length of a paragraph?

One sentence.

What's the fewest number of words you can have in a sentence?

One.

I never know how to end whatever I'm writing. What's the right way to do it?

We all know what it's like to have friends over for dinner. You finish eating, you sit around the living room for a while talking, and after you've yawned in their faces three or four times somebody finally says that maybe it's time to think about leaving. A while later everyone stands up, then half an hour later you're all standing near the door, your friends with their coats on, half asleep but still talking. It's amazing how long it takes some people to say good-bye. Likewise, it's amazing how long it takes some people to end a piece of writing. They keep going even though they've got nothing left to say.

We wrote back in Part Two that when you suddenly find yourself stuck, it's a signal that you might have the wrong outline. That's quite true. But when you suddenly find yourself stuck *after* you've covered all the points in your outline, it's a signal that you've reached your final destination. In this case, being stuck isn't at all a cause for concern; it's a cause for celebration. You've finished the job.

But don't I need to write a summary of some sort, or have a section with all my conclusions?

Not really. You can if you want to, and if it makes you happy go ahead. But if you've written a good draft and then polished it carefully, a section that summarizes your points or your conclusions will only repeat what you've already said. Your readers are busy, so why make them plow through the same stuff twice? It just isn't necessary. In other words, don't be afraid to end your piece of writing when you've said whatever it is you meant to say. This isn't a Fourth-of-July picnic; you don't need the literary equivalent of a fireworks display so that everyone will know the festivities are over. Let your piece of writing end naturally, and it will look just fine.

You mean you don't need a special sort of ending for a piece of writing? You just let it end wherever it happens to end?

That's exactly right, and to really hammer home this point we'll do it ourselves. You see, we've told you everything we know about how to write. We can't think of a single important point to add. So we'll wish you good luck, and without making a big deal about it we'll stop right here.